WAKING UP CATHOLIC

A Guide to Catholic Beliefs for
Converts, Reverts, and Anyone Becoming Catholic

By Chad R. Torgerson

Copyright

ISBN: 978-0-9895319-0-0
eISBN: 978-0-9895319-1-7

Assisi Media
530 Devonshire Lane, Unit 4
Crystal Lake, IL 60014
www.AssisiMedia.com

Permissions

Dedication

To my amazing wife, who always supported me in this adventure. I could not have done it without you. Marrying you was the best decision I have ever made, and I look forward to spending the rest of my life with you.

In loving memory of Thomas Nejmeh. You were my brother, my mentor, and my friend. Without you, my journey to Catholicism would have never begun. Your were the spark my faith needed to become a raging fire.

Acknowledgements

We would like to thank the following for helping to make this book a reality through their financial contributions:

The Nejmeh Family
The Hansen Family
The DeGuia Family
The Mateo Family
Jeff and Del Moses
Carl Bihler
Bob and Rena Wade
Donna Blizzard
Barbara Bridwell
Mimi Garcia
Barbara Henry
Alexis Martel
Donna O'Kane
Lee Potts
Tony Roybal
Joanne Teakles
Tami L. Wooliver
Tony and Carlotta Zuback
In loving memory of Alfonso Aleman
In honor of Our Lady of Guadalupe
In honor of Our Lady of Lourdes

Introduction

Childhood Dreams

Growing up, we often dream of our careers as adults and who we will become. I dreamt that one day I would wake up a policeman, a soldier, or a superhero. I did become a soldier, but the superhero idea might be difficult. Later in life after I became Christian, I dreamt of waking up as a youth minister, pastor, or missionary. My Protestant faith meant everything to me, so there is one thing I never dreamt of: *waking up Catholic*. I never thought that my life would lead me to the Catholic Church. I never thought that I would turn to Mary for her intercession or fall in love with the Eucharist. I never imagined praying the rosary or attending confession. While I never dreamt of this life, it still remains the best - and most important - decision that I have ever made.

Catholic Arithmetic

The journey to Catholicism can be scary for anyone seeking knowledge about the Church for the first time, or someone who has decided to return after years in the wilderness. Even someone who has been quietly sitting in the pews since childhood may have forgotten much of what he or she has learned. One of the greatest beauties of the Catholic faith is the depth of its teachings, but for someone without a graduate-level degree in theology, the average Catholic, it can be overwhelming. Naturally, we begin searching for answers. Looking online for answers can be difficult because we are unsure of whether those resources are trustworthy, and from my experience, many Catholic books read more like a college textbook than an invitation to the beauties of the Catholic faith. Personally, when I first began my journey to Catholicism, I struggled to find the answers to many questions. When I became Catholic, I wanted to ensure that others did not have the same experience.

When we want to teach children about mathematics, we do not begin with algebra, geometry, and advanced calculus; instead, we begin with basic arithmetic. We teach them how to count and that $1 + 1 = 2$. Before we can even get into multiplication, division, and fractions, we begin with the basics to build a strong foundation for their learning. Teaching Catholicism should follow the same model. Jumping into the depths of our theology too quickly will only turn people away. For instance, understanding how Catholic Tradition molds and shapes our faith, and how it works hand-in-hand with Sacred Scripture must be understood before we dive deeper into doctrines on the Virgin Mary, the saints, and the sacraments. We cannot become theologians until we understand the basics first.

Theology is a matter of the mind, but faith is a matter of the heart. With that in mind, my goal is to teach the basics of the faith in a way that is easy to understand - yet still pulls at your heart strings. Your mind will grasp the information, and your heart will thirst for more. By blending my own personal struggles during my faith journey with the basic teachings of Catholic theology, I hope that you will build the foundation that you need to grow and mature in faith.

Format of This Book

You are not alone in your struggles. Many concepts within Catholicism can be hard to grasp for a beginner. At the beginning of each chapter, I highlight some of the questions and issues I faced as I completed the RCIA process and beyond. Raised Lutheran, I fell away from Christianity for most of my teenage years until I finally accepted Christ as a young adult. For the next decade, I was a self-proclaimed, non-denominational Christian. These experiences shaped my views and biases against the Catholic Church. By exploring each of these biases, I can shed light on the errors in my understanding. My intentions were pure, but my direction was wrong. Knowing what led me there helped me to correct my course. I hope that it can do the same for you.

Acknowledging my misunderstanding of Catholic teaching was only the first step. The next step in the process was to find out what the Catholic Church *actually* taught. I quickly learned that my understanding of Catholicism was radically different from the Church's actual teachings. Exploring each topic, one by one, I began to have a better understanding of the Catholic faith, and I have tried to relay that information to you in a simple, easy-to-understand way. Taking quotations directly from Sacred Scripture (NAB translation), the *Catechism of the Catholic Church* (CCC), and the *United States Catholic Catechism for Adults* (USCCA), I have compiled the foundational teachings needed to begin a lifelong journey as a Catholic. Other books will cover these topics more thoroughly (and I encourage you to read them someday), but for now, let's simply focus on the central concepts of our religion.

Finally, after we have explored the misunderstandings of the Catholic faith and built a foundational understanding of the Church's teachings, the final step is to apply what we have learned to our daily life. *Knowing* the Word and *living* the Word are two entirely different things. The term *Catholic* is often used as a noun or adjective, but in reality, it is a state of being, a verb. Calling ourselves Catholic means little if we are not actively living out our faith. As each chapter comes to a close, and the book as a whole, I will help you to absorb the information you just learned and begin living it. We begin with participating in the Sacraments, praying earnestly to God, and eventually, sharing our newfound faith with the world around us. We finally become who Christ always meant us to be.

Catholics of All Levels

Who can benefit from a better understanding of the basics of the Catholic faith? Of course, the first people who come to mind are those who are exploring the Catholic faith for the first time. Society has profoundly skewed its perception of Catholicism, and *Waking Up Catholic* will help to shed light on the truth. The key to any journey is to know where you're going, and this book is the road map to get there. You do not have to worry about learning complex theological ideas; we are going to work our way from the ground up. We will start with a strong foundation and build from there. By the end of the book, you still may not be a theological scholar, but you will know what it truly means to be Catholic.

New Catholics can benefit tremendously from these chapters, but they are not the only ones. Many long-time Catholics have been sitting in the pews for years - unsure of what they actually believe. Others may not even attend Mass anymore, but Someone is calling them back home. Either way, they have likely forgotten much of what they learned from their childhood faith formation. Plus, many of those teachings may be blurred by what mainstream society and other Christian denominations teach about the faith. Does this describe you? Do you need a Catholic refresher course? Well, you have come to the right place. Here, you can be reminded of what makes the Catholic faith so incredible. If you have been away for awhile, this should be the first stop on your itinerary as you head back home.

Mature Catholics can also profit from these pages. Have you ever tried to share the faith with a non-Catholic? Have you ever attempted to encourage a fallen away Catholic to come back home? If you have, you have probably run into questions and arguments with Catholic doctrine. Sure, you can try using your favorite book on apologetics, trying to *argue* someone back home. Or you can learn to see the Church from their point-of-view: their objections, stumbling blocks, and concerns. By seeing the Church through their eyes, you can more lovingly share the faith in a way that will make sense to them. The greatest evangelists do not have the loudest voices; they have the softest ears. Listen to what people are saying, and use what you find in this book to open their hearts to new possibilities.

First Steps

For centuries, there have been some truly intelligent Catholic writers who have shaped our faith as we know it today. From St. Thomas Aquinas to G.K. Chesterton, your mind will overflow with the richness of the Catholic faith. Their works, however, can be a challenge to read, and if you are not ready for that yet, begin right here. Take the first steps towards becoming Catholic. Then, as you are ready to take your faith to a new level, I highly encourage you to continue reading these fantastic Catholic authors, as well as many of the other popular authors of today. The topics discussed here are just the tip of a very large iceberg, but remember, even Chesterton had to start somewhere.

Are you ready to begin?

Chapter 1
Tradition with a Capital *T*

From One Generation to the Next

Traditions passed down from one generation to the next have shaped the world that we know and see today. Many of the greatest differences between one society and another stem from the traditions that were passed down over many generations. With decades, centuries, and even millennia worth of traditions being passed down, the gaps between our different societies continue to widen. Even within the Christian church, the body of believers, large gaps have formed between the different denominations. Our differences continue to divide the church even further. Christ had envisioned one, unified church, but we have continued to find new ways to separate and divide ourselves. Catholic, Baptist, Methodist, and even non-denominational churches each have a core set of traditions to which they adhere, and they are often vastly different from one another. With the Catholic Tradition, *tradition* takes on a whole new meaning. Beyond the basic definition of tradition, the Catholic Tradition has become an integral part of how our faith as Catholics is formed. Despite our vast differences, can we come to a place where we are unified as one body of believers, the church Christ had envisioned?

My Life as a Protestant

Growing up in a Protestant church, I was raised to believe that there is only one source for finding out the truth about God: the Bible. This belief, known as *sola scriptura*, states that the only doctrine that we can follow must be found within the pages of the Bible. The term *sola scriptura* actually means "by scripture alone." So as a Protestant with this closely held belief, I had a difficult time with many of the teachings of the Catholic Church. Why do Catholics have seven Sacraments? Why do Catholics have such high regard for Mary? Who decides that a saint is a saint? I could not find a number of Catholic doctrines within the pages of the Bible. This left me confused and rather cynical toward the Church's teachings. The Catholic Church seemed to be making up rules as they went along, and it was the primary barrier between me and Catholicism.

I am one who enjoys a good debate. Debating Catholic Tradition with Catholics was always one of my favorite things to do. Of course, I usually felt as if I won the argument against my Catholic opponents who, in my opinion, seemed to know little about their own beliefs. In their defense, I have to admit that I was rarely ever listening. Instead of hearing what they had to say, I was always busy thinking of what doctrine I would question next. It was too easy. With a number of core tenets of the Catholic faith based on the Tradition of the Catholic Church, it was easy to point out that there were not any purely Biblical references for many of their beliefs. If they could not back it up with Scripture, I felt that their argument was null and void. The declarations or teachings from one pope, saint, or Catholic theologian mattered little to a Protestant like me. Debates can last for hours, but in the end, there was never actually a winner.

One of the things that amazed me most was the lack of knowledge that many Catholics had of their own beliefs. If you question some Catholics about why they believe in one doctrine or another, many of them cannot even tell you the reasons - they simply do. This very premise is one of the major inspirations of this book. If we, as Catholics, do not understand why we believe in certain doctrines, then how can we ever convince someone else of their merit? On the other hand, it is fantastic that Catholics believe and trust the Magisterium, the teaching body of the Church, so greatly. When pressed with an argument, many Catholics respond by saying that it is simply what they were taught; they do not question it. As a child, they learned the Catholic Tradition, and that is all they need to know. However, that may be sufficient for their own lives, but how can they truly spread the Word if they do not understand the basic tenets of their faith? It all begins with understanding the source of Catholic Tradition.

Understanding Catholic Tradition

The Sacred Tradition of the Catholic Church helps to form the basis of Catholic beliefs. Here, we use Tradition with a capital *T* because it refers to the official teachings of the Church, not just human traditions passed from one generation to the next. Along with Scripture, Tradition guides us and gives us the path to follow toward a closer relationship with Christ. The *Catechism of the Catholic Church*, quoting Pope Paul VI's *Dogmatic Constitution of Divine Revelation*, states:

> "*Sacred Tradition and Sacred Scripture, then, are bound closely together and communicate one with the other. For both of them, flowing out from the same divine well-spring, come together in some fashion to form one thing*

and move towards the same goal." -CCC 80, quoting Dei Verbum *9*

This statement describes how the Catholic Church views the Sacred Tradition as coming from the same source, God Himself, through the Holy Spirit. They are not the traditions set forth by man, but *the* Tradition that is inspired by the Lord.

Understanding that Catholicism encompasses both Scripture and Tradition, it begins to explain where many of the Catholic tenets come from. They do not see Scripture and Tradition as different forces but as two aspects of the same revelation of God. Tradition expands on the knowledge that we have from the Bible, and they work together to form a greater understanding. Much of Tradition can be traced back to the earliest days of the Church, found in the teachings and practices of the apostles and early Church fathers. Tradition itself continues to be unveiled as part of the revelation of God's love. Christ's revelation is complete, but our understanding of His revelation continues to grow and mature. As God is at work in our lives, His revelation continues to mold and inspire the Church toward a deeper faith. God's inspiration of man did not end with the canonization of the Bible; it continues in the evolution of the Church.

Long before printed pages, God came to man and shared His divine plan with us. This plan was passed down through the generations as part of the traditions of the Jewish faith. After Christ's resurrection, the stories and traditions of His life were passed down as a part of Tradition, as well. In time, these stories were combined to form the Scriptures that we know today.

The four Gospels and the rest of the New Testament were written down over time by those Apostles and others associated with them who worked under the inspiration of the Holy Spirit. -USCCA, page 26

They were inspired by the Holy Spirit; the same Holy Spirit who lives and dwells within us today. After Christ's death and resurrection, the Apostles continued His teaching. This continued as part of the oral Tradition.

What Jesus said and did, the Apostles preached to others. They brought to their preaching a deeper understanding of what they had experienced, having been instructed by the events of Christ's life and enlightened by the Holy Spirit. - USCCA, page 26 (cf. CCC, no. 126, citing DV, no. 19)

Even after Christ's life, the Holy Spirit continued to inspire the leaders of the Church, the Apostles. Just as the Apostles were inspired two thousand years ago, the Spirit continues to inspire the leaders of the Church today.

The combination of the Scriptures and Tradition gives us a better look at the whole message of God. To ignore Sacred Tradition, we would be missing out on the teachings that He has given to the leaders of our Church. Our line of popes, along with our local bishops, priests, and deacons, have been a crucial part of forming the foundations of our Church over the centuries. They have fed us with Scripture and challenged us with the Tradition. Sacred Tradition is integrated into many aspects of the Catholic faith, and it would be difficult to imagine the Church without it. Without it, our faith would ultimately not be complete. Christ has given us Tradition, along with the Scriptures, to give us a guide on how we should form our faith.

Inspired by the Holy Spirit

Sola scriptura focuses on the Bible as the one source of faith because it is the inspired Word of God. It was written by the apostles and their immediate followers through the revelation of the Holy Spirit. Catholics believe that Christ's revelation is complete; we simply continue to understand, teach, and define it through Catholic Tradition. Many Protestants, non-Catholics, and even Catholics question the authority of the leaders in the Catholic Church to define Tradition. What gives them the authority? It is the same authority that gave the early Christian teachers and writers the authority to share the message of Christ. Through Sacred Tradition, this authority has been passed down, from one generation to the next, to continue sharing the Divine Law. Instead of questioning the authority of the Catholic leaders, Protestants and non-Catholics should question *sola scriptura*. Why would God not continue to inspire our Christian leaders?

The Apostles, the early Church leaders, were a group of men that were called to ministry. They helped to form the foundation of the Church. From this foundation, they would share the Good News with the world. After His resurrection, Jesus called them to this mission.

> *Then Jesus approached and said to them, "All power in heaven and on earth has been given to me. Go, therefore, and make disciples of all nations, baptizing them in the name of the Father, and of the Son, and of the holy Spirit, teaching them to observe all that I have commanded you. And behold, I am with you always, until the end of the age." -Matthew 28:18-20, NAB*

This command that Jesus gave to His disciples is called the Great Commission. Here, He tells them to continue what He had started. Christ's death and resurrection were not the end of the Christian story; it was only the beginning.

At Pentecost, just weeks after Christ's resurrection, the Holy Spirit came down to fill the Apostles.

> *And suddenly there came from the sky a noise like a strong driving wind, and it filled the entire house in which they were. Then there appeared to them tongues as of fire, which parted and came to rest on each one of them. And they were all filled with the holy Spirit and began to speak in different tongues, as the Spirit enabled them to proclaim. -Acts 2: 2-4, NAB*

God Himself entered these men in the form of the Holy Spirit. From that moment on, the Apostles began their mission to spread the Gospel. With the power of the Holy Spirit, these men were spreading the true Word of God. It is that same Spirit that lives within us today, including in the current leaders of the Catholic Church.

If Christ wanted us to follow the *sola scriptura* belief, He would have told the Apostles to write down all that they had heard and tell others to read it, but He wanted them to do more than that. They were given the Holy Spirit so that they could continue sharing Christ's message verbally, even after He was gone. Beyond the Gospels, the rest of the New Testament is based on the teachings of the early Church leaders. A majority of those writings came from St. Paul, a man who only converted to Christianity after spending much of his life persecuting early Christians. Despite not being one of Christ's first followers, a number of his letters and writings were included in the New Testament anyway. Without a doubt, this proves that the Spirit inspired and moved the teachers of the early Church, just as they continue to be moved today.

Inspired by the Holy Spirit, the leaders of the Church have refined how we look at our faith. Our daily walk with Christ has been molded by the words of great men, but these great men could not have done it alone. After Christ's Ascension to heaven, they began by giving us the inspired Word of God through the oral form of Tradition; only years later did they continue through the written Scriptures. Christ called us through the Great Commission and empowered us at Pentecost. It began with the Apostles, and it remains true for us today. Just as the Apostles were inspired, so too are the leaders of today's Catholic Church.

Passing the Tradition

Throughout the Old Testament, we can see God's work in the lives of the Jewish people. He was not simply present at the Garden with Adam and Eve. He did not disappear after He made the covenant with Abraham. Even after He led Moses and the chosen people to the Promised Land, He remained in their lives. So, why would He leave us after bringing us a New Covenant through Christ's sacrifice on the cross? He did not leave us. Instead, God came down in the form of the Holy Spirit to be with us always. The last canonized book of the Bible may have been written almost two thousand years ago, but God's interaction in our lives continues. And just as He commissioned the Apostles two thousand years ago, He continues to commission our leaders today.

From the beginning, Christ knew the importance of giving the Church the authority to lead Christians. In the Gospel of Matthew, Christ discusses the authority that the Church possesses. When telling a fellow Christian that he or she has sinned, we should approach him or her ourselves in private. If that does not work, then we should involve one or two others. Then, when that fails, we turn to the Church for guidance:

> *"If he refuses to listen to them, tell the church. If he refuses to listen even to the church, then treat him as you would a Gentile or a tax collector. Amen, I say to you, whatever you bind on earth shall be bound in heaven, and whatever you loose on earth shall be loosed in heaven." -Matthew 18:17-18, NAB*

Jesus clearly states that the Church has authority here on earth. And when He is speaking to them, He is not saying that only the Apostles had this authority, but the Church as a whole. The Church itself had not even been established as it is today, but Christ gave this commandment to His disciples knowing the Church to come.

Can you describe your life in less than a paragraph? Can you easily define your mission in life? How do you see yourself? In the Catechism of the Catholic Church, we can see how the Church sees itself.

> *The Church, "the pillar and bulwark of the truth," faithfully guards "the faith which was once for all delivered to the saints." She guards the memory of Christ's words; it is she who from generation to generation hands on the apostles' confession of faith.   -CCC 171, quoting 1 Timothy 3:15 and Jude 3*

The "pillar and bulwark of the truth," taken from 1 Timothy 3:15, is a Scripture reference where the Church can find its purpose. Guarding Christ's message, the Church passes down the teachings of the Apostles to each new generation. If *sola scriptura* states that we should believe the Bible is wholly true, then we should acknowledge the truth of the Church that is passed down from one generation to the next. By downplaying the role of the Church, *sola scriptura* somewhat contradicts itself. We must realize that it is a combination of Scripture and Sacred Tradition that fully encompasses Christ's message in a living, breathing Church.

Tradition's Impact

How does Catholic Tradition impact our lives? In what ways does it mold our belief system? There are a number of teachings that are significantly impacted by Catholic Tradition. One need only to look at the seven sacraments. Penance, Anointing of the Sick, and even the Eucharistic belief in transubstantiation are based on the combination of Scripture and Tradition. In fact, the Catholic Tradition will continue to be a key theme throughout this book. With the Sacred Tradition being the major dividing factor between Catholics and non-Catholics, many of the differences will arise from this distinction. Therefore, to understand the Catholic view on these subjects as found later in this book, it is vital to understand the concept of Catholic Tradition. Without it as a cornerstone of belief, it would be difficult to understand the Catholic view on many subjects.

Beyond the larger topics of the Sacraments, such as our views on Mary, the saints, papal authority, and the priesthood, Catholic Tradition impacts us in other ways, as well. The way we practice our faith from day to day is directly impacted by Tradition. For instance, observing Lent is a common part of Catholic Tradition. Although many other denominations also observe Lent, many do not. One example of a major difference between the Catholic observance of Lent and other denominations is the practice of giving up meat on Fridays. For Catholics, Lent is a time of fasting and prayer - growing closer to God through contemplative prayer and strengthening our bond with Him through sacrifice. Other denominations do not observe these practices, and they are missing out on real opportunities for growth through penance and sacrifice. Following Catholic Tradition allows us to practice our faith in ways that push the limits of our faith. Lent is an excellent example of that.

Whether from Scripture or Tradition, a number of practices are designed to draw us nearer to God. Observing Lent is one example. Regularly confessing our sins in the Sacrament of Penance, participating in the Eucharist, and attending Mass are also practices that should enrich our faith. The challenges we face in these practices are not to hold us down but to uplift us. They may differ from the beliefs found in other denominations, but they are the beauty of the Catholic faith. In my short time as a Catholic, I now embrace the Tradition that I once ridiculed. I have seen the effect that it has on my life, and the new depths that it has brought to my faith. Never have I felt as close to God as I do now as a Catholic.

A New View of Tradition

As someone who grew up in the Protestant church, Catholic Tradition had always been a source of debate. Always looking for Scriptural reference, it just never made any sense to me. Through my studies of Catholic Tradition, my mind began to change, and I started to understand the basic premise of Sacred Tradition. My ignorance and stubbornness led me to misconceptions, but with an open heart, I started to see Tradition as the Word of God passed down orally through the generations. After practicing the Catholic faith, I could finally see the impact that it had on my life.

We often mock what we do not understand, and no one is more guilty of that than I am. For years, I misunderstood the Catholic faith - and the Tradition that helps to form it. It separated me from the Catholic Church, just as it has divided and separated Christ's church for centuries. For me, that time is over. Others may choose not to follow the Catholic faith, but I have found beauty in the Catholic Church. Either way, it is time for us to find unity in Christ despite our many differences. We may choose to practice our faith in a number of different ways, but we are all one body of believers in Christ. I pray that you can find the same beauty that I have found in the Catholic Tradition, but if you do not, as a Christian, I am proud to call you my brothers and sisters in Christ.

Chapter 2
Guardians of the Faith

I Don't Play Well With Others

Growing up, I was not exactly a part of the social elite. I was a shy, awkward kid and did not have many friends. My imagination kept me company, most days, and life was pretty simple. Without all of the social pressures of trying to fit in with the crowd, it was easy just to be me, regardless of what people thought of me. As I grew older, nothing changed. I still had no interest in adhering to social norms - including any form of religion or theological beliefs. Call me an atheist. Call me agnostic. It didn't actually matter to me. Beyond simply rejecting belief in God, I rejected the need for the hierarchy of the Church. To me, it was just another crowd that I would never quite fit into.

Years later, after converting to Christianity, I had found a need for God; however, I still felt no need for the leaders of the Church. During my conversion, I had found Christianity on my own. I did not need the Church then; why would I need it now? Everything we ever need to know about God, so I thought, could be found in the Bible. Of course, that was before I understood the Sacred Tradition. Without the Sacred Tradition, there was no need for the hierarchy of the Church to maintain it. Without the Church, there was no Sacred

Tradition. One canceled out the other, and vice versa. It was easy to see where the Protestant idea of *sola scriptura* came from. There was a co-dependency between the Church and Sacred Tradition; eliminate one, and you eliminate both of them. Before long, I became a card-carrying, Bible-believing Christian. It was just me and God; I thought that was all I ever needed.

Just "Christian"

Man as a species has an unending urge to put a name or label on things. From the time that God first asked Adam to name all of the animals, we have not stopped putting a label on everything we could. Have you ever been in a relationship without a label on it? Until you can call each other boyfriend, girlfriend, fiancé, husband, or wife, it is not really official. Somehow, without a label, it is just not real to us. So as a new Christian, the first question people asked me was, "What denomination are you?" To which, I replied, "None. I'm *just Christian*." Just Christian? In my mind, I did not want to be bound by the thought of some group of old men and women deciding what I should believe or not believe. Belief, for me, was a personal choice, and the Bible was a matter of personal interpretation. I didn't need anyone to tell me anything different, and that was that.

Even though I tried to avoid it, labels still followed me. Explaining my theological beliefs to people over and over again grew tiresome. In time, I began to tell people that I was non-denominational, but in the truest sense of the word, of course. While most non-denominational Christians begin to fall into this blurry line between what is and isn't a denomination (do 40,000 people at a single Church become a denomination?), my beliefs, from my perspective, were purer than that. There was not a church or denomination on this entire planet that I "followed." I may have attended certain churches, but I never followed. Looking back, I was kidding myself. While I thought that I was a Christian rebel, I believed in the same mainstream Christian philosophies as everyone else. In the end, only one label truly fit - *hypocrite*.

Anything But Catholic

Labels will eventually catch up to you. I had tried extremely hard not to put labels on my faith; however, society's norms crept in. I labeled myself as a *non-denominational Christian*, but it didn't bother me. As long as I was practicing my faith in ways that I enjoyed I decided that labels didn't matter. Contemporary music and worship services coupled with feel-good teachings and sermons were my idea of a good Sunday. Growing up Lutheran, I had my taste of a more traditional service, and it was difficult just to stay awake. The services held at more modern churches suited my needs better. Whenever I was faced with finding a new church because of a move or simply on a whim, it had to be a contemporary church. Old-fashioned services like the ones I grew up with were just not my style - especially Catholic services. It was the same thing, week in, week out. Don't Catholics get bored?

The "entertainment value" of many modern churches could be an entire chapter itself, but my true problem with old-fashioned churches stemmed from my view of their leadership. They seemed out of touch with the rest of society. Contemporary churches had embraced modern music and styles. The Catholic Church had made claims to being relevant in the modern world, but they still clung to the same traditions. Personally, I thought that holding onto old traditions and staying relevant could not coexist. Catholic services felt tired and plain. Modern services left me feeling vibrant and alive. So, when it came to finding a new church, I would try just about anything - anything but Catholic, that is.

Old men in long robes just could not hold a candle to a young, hip pastor in a pair of jeans and a shirt with the sleeves rolled up. How could I relate to the pope? Who was this guy that millions of people hung on his every word? And, who are the guys with him? What's the difference between a bishop, priest, and deacon anyway? The Catholic hierarchy confused me, and life seemed much simpler following the local pastor. Convincing me to become Catholic would be no minor feat, and this was one of the first steps. Most of my opposition to the Church came from my opposition to Sacred Tradition, and Sacred Tradition relied on Church leadership. I'm not a follower, never have been; it was going to take some pretty strong arguments to convince me to start following now.

Meeting the Pope

No, I have never actually met the pope (wouldn't that be a memorable moment?), yet, as my curiosity about Catholicism began, I knew that I needed to know as much about him as possible. How did he get his position? In fact, what is his position, and why does it exist? What does it mean to be *infallible*? Can he truly never be wrong? There was so much to learn, and I still did not understand everything I truly needed to know. What I did learn is that one simple act by Christ himself was the basis of it all. In a passage that I had read many times, I had never noticed its significance. Now, with the guidance of Catholic doctrine, I began to see the Pope in an entirely different way.

In the Gospel of Matthew, Chapter 16, Jesus was teaching His disciples a lesson, when it seemed, in my mind, to dawn on Him that they were not understanding what He was saying. The disciples had seen many of Jesus' miraculous signs and heard many of His teachings; however, they still seemed lost. Ensuring that they truly understood whom He was, Jesus decided to ask His disciples directly.

> *When Jesus went into the region of Caesarea Philippi, he asked his disciples, "Who do people say that the Son of Man is?" They replied, "Some say John the Baptist, others Elijah, still others Jeremiah or one of the prophets." He said to them, "But who do you say that I am?" Simon Peter said in reply, "You are the Messiah, the Son of the living God."*
> *Jesus said to him in reply, "Blessed are you, Simon son of Jonah. For flesh and blood has not revealed this to you, but my heavenly Father." -Matthew 16:13-17, NAB*

Simon Peter's response was exactly what Jesus was hoping for. Jesus wanted to know if the disciples understood whom He was, and Simon Peter stepped up to represent them with his answer. Answering this one simple question, Simon Peter put into motion a series of events that shaped the foundation of the Catholic Church.

The story does not end with Jesus calling Simon Peter "blessed." Furthering His response to Simon Peter, Jesus continues:

> *"And so I say to you, you are Peter, and upon this rock I will build my church, and the gates of the netherworld shall not prevail against it. I will give you the keys to the kingdom of heaven. Whatever you bind on earth shall be bound in heaven; and whatever you loose on earth shall be loosed in heaven." -Matthew 16:18-19, NAB*

Verse by verse, let's look at this passage. It begins with definitively saying Jesus Christ's role in the world as the Messiah, the Son of God and the Son of Man. This is led by Peter boldly, and without hesitation, answering Jesus' question. Peter led the disciples in proclaiming Christ's glory in this moment, and he would continue to do so for the rest of his life.

Next, Jesus tells Peter that he is blessed to understand Christ's true identity. When Jesus asked who people thought He was, the disciples named some of the Bible's greatest prophets. When Jesus asked them who *they* thought He was, it was Peter that spoke first. Peter's understanding of how Jesus fulfilled the Old Testament prophecies was key, and it was one reason that he would take his role as the first pope. Nobody told Peter what to say - not even Jesus. God had revealed this to Peter; it shows his openness to God's guidance and will. Peter had the makings of a great leader. The Father knew it. Jesus knew it. But did Peter? Did the other disciples?

When Jesus spoke to Simon and called him "Peter," it helps to understand why He would do such a thing. In its original Aramaic, Peter meant "rock," so Jesus was saying, "You are (*Rock*), and upon this *rock* I will build my church." Understanding this became a turning point in my conversion to Catholicism. As a Protestant and non-denominational Christian, I obviously understood the significance of the role that the disciples and Apostles played, but I had never before caught the true importance of this verse. Jesus was publicly declaring the special position that Peter would hold within the Church - a Church that did not even exist yet.

In the next line of that verse, Jesus tells Peter, "I will give you the keys to the kingdom of heaven. Whatever you bind on earth shall be bound in heaven; and whatever you loose on earth shall be loosed in heaven" (Matthew 16:19, NAB). As you will learn later in this book, this sets the stage for priestly duties, such as hearing confessions that the Apostles would one day carry out as the original leaders of the Church, but note that the keys were given directly to Peter. For this reason, we, as Catholics, believe that Peter, and his successors - the popes - had the final word within the Church. It was true 2,000 years ago, and it still holds true today.

The Apostles

Let's begin by defining "who are the apostles, and what was their role?" Again, let's turn to Scripture for the answer:

In those days he departed to the mountain to pray, and he spent the night in prayer to God. When day came, he called his disciples to himself, and from them he chose Twelve, whom he also named apostles: Simon, whom he named Peter, and his brother Andrew, James, John, Philip, Bartholomew, Matthew, Thomas, James the son of Alphaeus, Simon who was called a Zealot, and Judas the son of James, and Judas Iscariot, who became a traitor. - Luke 6:12-16, NAB

To quickly answer the question, twelve of Jesus' closest disciples, were named as His apostles. They were not chosen for their positions in religious society; they were fishermen, a Zealot (rebel), and even a tax collector - ordinary men (and sinners) from all walks of life - yet they were chosen as the first leaders of the Church. Their goal: carry on the missionary work of Christ.

The apostles were sent out by Jesus to continue spreading His teachings. Jesus was already having an impact everywhere He went, but this allowed His message to spread even further. Of course, after Christ's death and Resurrection, they would continue with the mission of spreading the Gospel.

In keeping with the Lord's command, the Gospel was handed on in two ways:
-orally "by the apostles who handed on, by the spoken word of their preaching, by the example they gave, by the institutions they established, what they themselves had received - whether from the lips of Christ, from his way of life and his works, or whether they had learned it at the prompting of the Holy Spirit"
-in writing "by those apostles and other men associated with the apostles who, under the inspiration of the same Holy Spirit, committed the message of salvation to writing." -CCC, 76, quoting Dei Verbum *7*

This passage from the Catechism teaches us about the two primary ways of spreading the Gospel - orally and in writing. Of course, this mission would not end with the original twelve. If Christ's message was to be carried on, it had to be passed down.

Successors of the Apostles

Christ did not come to save one generation of people from a select part of the world; He came to save all generations from all nations. To accomplish this, it meant that His message could not end with the original apostles. Only by passing the Gospel down, both orally and in written form, could it continue to make a difference 2,000 years later. By appointing successors to the apostles, men entrusted to carry on the mission of the original twelve, the Church could continue to grow, in number and geographically. If it is God's goal to bring Christ's salvation to all nations and all generations, then the successors to the apostles are the key to making it happen.

Searching for Biblical evidence of apostolic succession does not take long. In Acts 1, just after Jesus' death and resurrection, the apostles - led by Peter - immediately sought to replace Judas (who had hung himself after betraying Jesus). The decision was between two men, Justus and Matthias.

> Then they gave lots to them, and the lot fell upon Matthias, and he was counted with the eleven apostles. - Acts 1:26, NAB

Matthias was chosen, by casting lots, to fill the position Judas once held. This tradition of the apostles succeeding one another has continued for the last two millennia, and today, we know them better as our bishops and archbishops.

As the Church grew, the hierarchy grew, as well. Bishops took charge of larger geographical areas that we now know as dioceses and archdioceses. They appointed priests to be the heads of local congregations, or parishes, and assigned deacons as helpers to both the bishops and priests. Evidence of this goes all the way back to the New Testament. All three positions are mentioned numerous times and can be found in Timothy, Titus, and other New Testament books. The Catholic Church's hierarchy was not some system drummed up centuries later; it was in place from the very beginning of the Church. Understanding the Biblical significance of the leaders of the Catholic Church gave me a whole new perspective on the Church as a whole.

The Pope: Bishop of Rome

We learned about Peter's special place in the history of the Church. We also learned about the successors of the apostles, the bishops. Putting these two ideas together, we can better understand the role of the pope. Peter, like the other apostles, would eventually be succeeded by another bishop. Peter was the Bishop of Rome, where he served alongside Paul. This office, the Bishop of Rome, has taken a significant place within the Church ever since that time. Each successor of the Bishop of Rome takes Peter's place and is regarded to as the leader of the Catholic Church, whom we affectionately call the pope. This line of successors, which can be traced back from Peter until now, leads us to our current pope, Pope Francis.

History can quickly fade, and we are often unsure about events that happened only a few hundred years ago. Somehow, despite other flaws in recorded history, the Catholic Church can name each one of the popes. This is by no accident. There has been constant leadership in the Church from the beginning, and dedicated efforts were taken to preserve the teachings of the Church. Most Protestant churches only date back the last two hundred years or so, and the earliest Protestants date back only to the 16th century. Meanwhile, the Catholic Church can trace its line of leaders all the way back to Peter himself. Jesus gave the keys to the Kingdom of Heaven directly to Peter, and those keys have been passed down, generation to generation, from one pope to the next. I had once thought that the Catholic hierarchy, including the pope, was no longer relevant. Now, I realized that the papacy was more than relevant; it was timeless.

The Church and Sacred Tradition

In Chapter 1, we learned about the role of Sacred Tradition in the Church. Without it, many other Catholic teachings can become hard to explain through *sola scriptura*. In this chapter, we learned about Peter and the apostles, their successors, and their role of preserving the teaching of the Church through the Magisterium. The Magisterium, by the way, is the official teaching authority of the Church, comprised of the pope and bishops. It was designed to protect everything we know about our faith. Now, we can bring these two ideas together. While much of the foundation of the Church can be found in Scripture, Sacred Tradition has helped to shape and refine the nature of the Church. In return, the Church has served as the guardian of the Sacred Tradition and has assured its accuracy from the beginning. Together, they define the Church; they are what separates us from other Christian traditions. No other denomination has the rich history and long-standing teachings like the Catholic Church. This was reason enough for me to fall head-over-heels in love with Catholicism.

On their own, the Church and its Sacred Tradition can be criticized and picked apart by naysayers of Catholicism. Together, they hold firm. Together, they build an impenetrable fortress of reason and logic. As we begin to study and learn about the Catholic faith, we must always keep these two at the center of our studies. They will guide us in the right direction and show us a deeper level of Christianity than we will find anywhere else. I had always considered myself a student of Christianity, but opening myself up to Catholicism, this beautiful faith protected by the bishops, priests, and deacons, has shown me more than I had ever known before. The more I learn, the more I want to learn.

The Relevant Church

My entire life, I was an outsider - never truly fitting in with the rest of the crowd. Now, as a Catholic, especially as Catholicism is under attack in the United States, I find myself an outsider again. For so many years, I had rejected the Catholic faith because I did not want to be a part of the *establishment.* I wanted to be a free-thinker and did not want old men in fancy robes telling me what to do. Instead, I turned to the classroom and everything science could teach me; I turned to society to learn what was socially acceptable; I turned to preachers in blue jeans to find wisdom. I thought I was radical, but now, I realize that the men standing at the altar adoring the Eucharist are the true radicals. It is the men and women who devote their lives to God and live chastely that are radicals. And it is the Catholics around the world, standing up for what they believe - regardless of what society may say - that are radicals.

Fifteen years ago, I was blessed to find Jesus. He changed my life. From that point on, I knew that Jesus was real and relevant in my life, and I wanted to find a church that was just as relevant. I thought that I needed to find a church with modern music and even more modern teachings. I thought that giant auditoriums would bring huge relevance to my life. I thought wrong. When I struggled to find a relevant church, the last place I thought of looking was the Catholic Church; however, when I finally opened up to it, I found a Church that was as timeless as it was relevant. If Jesus is timeless, why can't the Church be? Open your heart to the Catholic Church. When you allow the leaders of the Church, the successors of the apostles, to guide you, you will be amazed by the wisdom they share. For any organization to survive 2,000 years, it is a miracle. The Church, guided by its leaders, has survived for one reason alone: because through Christ, it was, is, and always will be relevant.

Chapter 3
Shepherds of the Flock

Blue Jeans and Fancy Robes

Every Christian denomination has its form of priests. Some call them pastors, teachers, ministers, or even bishops. Regardless of what we may call them, they seem to fulfill the same primary purpose: shepherd the flock of the local congregation. Some wear robes; others think it's cool to wear blue jeans and an un-ironed dress shirt with the sleeves rolled up. In some denominations, the preachers, priests, and ministers scare us with tales of fire and brimstone. Other churches like to focus on Jesus, our *buddy*, who will bring financial security and deliverance from hard times. Their messages differ as greatly as their wardrobes. As good Christians, how do we know whom to follow?

As a young man finding Christianity for the first time, little appealed to me about old men in long robes. I quickly found my way into more contemporary churches with the bright lights, loud music, and Bible-based teachings. It felt like a home away from home - a place where you called everyone brother and sister. Each week, I felt re-energized with my faith and ready to take on the world. Following these modern preachers just felt natural to me. They were utterly devoted to their ministries, and I aspired to be just like them. In my mind, they embodied what it truly meant to be a devoted Christian.

My Own Flock

When I first became Christian, I rejected any form of religious authority (look back to Chapter 2 on Catholic authority to find out more), but over time, I began to see how a faithful preacher with a message could have a positive impact on people, including me. It inspired me to begin working with the youth at my local church. At first, because I had little experience, I spent my days teaching 4 year-olds stories from the Bible. I spent more time cleaning spills than teaching the Gospel. Eventually, I decided that I wanted to do more, and I began assisting the young adults ministry aimed at the twenty-something crowd. As a twenty-something myself, I served as a peer leader in the group.

The youth minister at that church noticed my ability to lead the group and asked me to host a weekly event for the ministry. Each week, I got up on stage and introduced speakers, bands, and other guests while doing a little teaching myself. Growing up as a shy, awkward kid, I never would have imagined myself in this position, but somehow, I felt right at home. Put me in a crowded room alone, and I will hide somewhere in the corner. Put me on stage with a microphone, and I feel like I could light up the room. This youth minister, who was not much older than I was, gave me a unique opportunity to find a gift that I never thought existed.

I was inspired. The opportunity to help lead people to Christ excited me. At the time, I felt that I had found my calling. Part of me would have been happy to simply go into youth ministry, but part of me felt called to do more. I was convinced that I should go to seminary and become a non-

SHEPHERDS OF THE FLOCK

denominational pastor. Tending someone else's flock was fun, but how much greater would it be to have a flock of my own? I researched the process of becoming a pastor and enrolled myself in an online Bible college. My plan was set. In a few short years, I would be ready to lead a flock of my own.

Dedication

What does it take to become a Christian minister, pastor, or religious leader? Well, it varies across denominations. Some denominations are pretty strict, such as the Catholic Church, and require a pretty lengthy process. Others are not as strict. With a Bachelor's degree, I could begin working as a youth minister; with a Master's in Divinity or Theology, I could lead a church of my own. Regardless of the educational or other requirements, I lacked the most crucial aspect of a life devoted to God: dedication. Life threw a few curve balls at me, including a military deployment to Kuwait, and I quickly fell off track. My life as a Christian pastor was put on hold - indefinitely.

As life tossed me around like a small rowboat on stormy seas, I struggled to stay focused on my calling. Like most people, I spent most of my time just trying to survive and lost track of what I was truly called to do. My lack of real dedication stopped me from pursuing ministry any further. Looking back, I can see how God had a plan in all of this. It may have seemed that my dreams of spreading the faith were gone, but my time simply had not come yet. One day, an opportunity to share my faith would come again, and in a very unexpected place - the Catholic Church.

Giving Up

My life ultimately led me to the Catholic Church (as you obviously already know), and one of the most difficult aspects of that journey was my willingness to give up my call to ministry. The Catholic Church had strict requirements for entering the religious life, and a primary requirement for most positions (excluding deacons) was to remain unmarried. At the time I entered the Church, I was already in a long-term relationship that I was not ready to give up with a woman who is now my wife. Other than becoming a deacon at some point, it meant giving up ministry. I was faced with a decision: pursue my dream of full-time ministry or follow where God was leading me - the Catholic Church. In the end, I decided to follow God and began the RCIA process to become Catholic.

Giving up my dreams of going into ministry saddened me. I struggled to understand why I could not serve the Church as a married man. Why did it have to be one or the other? Did God not want me to share my faith anymore? Why had He given me these gifts? I had more questions than answers. To find the answers I was looking for, I realized that I needed to understand more about the Catholic religious life, and how it impacted me. Before I could fully give my allegiance to Catholicism, I needed to know where I would fit in the Church. I wanted to do more than faithfully sit in a pew each week; I wanted to be on the front lines for the battle of souls. Little did I know, that dream was not lost yet.

Call No Man "Father"

The Catholic Church is full of titles that seemed strange to me, at first. We call men in the religious life *father* and *brother*; we call religious women *mother* and *sister*; yet none of them have any real relation to us. They hold positions of authority within the Church, but we call them by family names. As a Christian convert, I was not entirely surprised by these titles. In Matthew 23, we learn:

> *"As for you, do not be called 'Rabbi.' You have but one teacher, and you are all brothers." -Matthew 23:8, NAB*

This seems straightforward enough, but I struggled with the continuation of that verse:

> *"Call no one on earth your father; you have but one Father in heaven." -Matthew 23:9, NAB*

How, then, could Catholics refer to their priests as *father*. I have a biological father on earth, and God the Father in Heaven. It seemed wrong to call priests *father*, so I decided to learn a little more.

The first part of this teaching, referring to each other in familial ways, is not difficult to understand. As a Church, we are one extended family united in the faith. We share a common love of our Lord, Jesus Christ, and it bonds us in ways that could only be compared to our biological families. Together, we share one Father in Heaven, thus making us all children of God. We are brothers and sisters in Christ. Few Christians would argue with these statements. Where things begin to differ is when we use them as titles, such as in the Catholic Church. Yes, we are brothers and sisters, but Jesus also commanded us to call no man *father*.

My Protestant background taught me that it was wrong to call priests father, but according to this verse, it would seem that the same should be true for my biological father, as well. How can we call any man our father, dad, daddy, pa, or other similar name? Should these not be used? How can we apply this verse to the leaders of our spiritual families but not our biological families? For me, understanding came when I stopped reading the text literally and started listening for what Jesus was trying to tell me. He was not warning us against using specific titles themselves, but what those titles represented.

There is but one God, one Father in Heaven. All praise and glory should go to Him alone. However, we can begin to lose sight of that. Some of our spiritual leaders in this world make such an impact in our lives that we begin to praise them also. Look at many televangelists with thousands, if not millions, of followers, and you will see that people have begun to idolize them. This was Jesus' concern. He was warning against making gods of mortal men - not of the words we choose to call someone. In other words, it is okay to call a man our spiritual father, as long as we do not give him the praise only our Father in Heaven should receive.

This was a sound theory, but was there any Biblical evidence to support it? Did the early Christians call anyone father? In fact, they did. St. Paul refers to himself as the Corinthians' spiritual father:

> *I am writing you this not to shame you, but to admonish you as my beloved children. Even if you should have countless guides to Christ, yet you do not have many fathers, for I became your father in Christ Jesus through the gospel. -1 Corinthians 4:14-15, NAB*

There are numerous other examples of how St. Paul sees his followers, including Timothy, as his children. St. Paul, the great writer of a number of books in the New Testament, defined his relationship in this way many times. Just as St. Paul was the spiritual father to many early Christians, our local priests serve as spiritual fathers to our parishes. What began in the beginning of the Church continues today.

In all of St. Paul's writings, he never asked anyone to honor him for his teachings or charitable works; in fact, he did just the opposite - continually giving glory to God the Father. He obviously saw no problem in relating to Timothy and others as a parent would a child, as well. So, we can model the relationships we have with our priests and religious leaders the same way. They can be our spiritual fathers, brothers, and sisters, as long as we do not begin to inappropriately give them the praise that only God deserves. With that understanding, I was finally able to see those men in long robes, who liked to be called father, in a new light.

The Common Priesthood

Growing up as a Protestant, I never felt the need for a mediator between God and me. If I wanted to talk to God, I did so through prayer. When it came to my salvation, I found God without the help of a priest, and I surely did not feel one was necessary now. My life had entirely changed, and all I needed was Christ in my life. God loves me. What else could I possibly need? What could someone offer me that I could not get directly from God Himself? St. Peter tells us:

> *Come to him, a living stone, rejected by human beings but chosen and precious in the sight of God, and, like living stones, let yourselves be built into a spiritual house to be a holy priesthood to offer spiritual sacrifices acceptable to God through Jesus Christ. -1 Peter 2:4-5, NAB*

As St. Peter tells us in this verse, we, as Christians, are part of a holy priesthood. Why, then, does the Catholic Church have its own established priesthood?

Does the Catholic Church deny that we are part of the priesthood? No. The Church, in fact, teaches that we are all part of the common priesthood as described in 1 Peter 2. If we are all part of the common priesthood, how do we differ from priests? Well, priests, bishops, and deacons fall under what the Church calls the ministerial priesthood - those conferred by the Sacrament of Holy Orders:

> *The ministerial priesthood differs in essence from the common priesthood of the faithful because it confers a sacred power for the service of the faithful. The ordained ministers exercise their service for the People of God by teaching* (munus docendi*), divine worship* (munus liturgicum*), and pastoral governance* (munus regendi*). - CCC, 1592*

In simpler terms, the ministerial priesthood teaches us, leads us in worship, and guides us as a Church.

Each of these roles has been vital to the success of the Church for the past 2,000 years. They serve as guardians of the Truth when serving as our teachers. They administer the Sacraments, keeping them holy, when leading us in worship of our Most High God. And as the leaders of the Catholic Church, their guidance and governance have helped us to remain strong as a religious community, even as the Church spreads to the furthest corners of the globe. Without good leadership, any organization would fail. Our priesthood, endowed with a sacred power through the Sacrament of Holy Orders, provides the leadership we need to thrive.

Holy Orders and the Religious Life

The Catholic Church is full of different titles: the pope, cardinals, bishops, priests, deacons, religious sisters, and monks (religious brothers). When converting to Catholicism, understanding how these different roles fit into the hierarchy of the Church can be extremely confusing, but it's not as difficult as it appears. Basically, we can break it down into those who have become part of the ministerial priesthood, through the Sacrament of Holy Orders, and those who have consecrated their lives to Christ. Bishops (including the pope and cardinals), priests, and deacons are part of the ministerial priesthood. Religious brothers and sisters, meanwhile, have simply (or not so simply) consecrated - completely dedicated - their lives to Christ.

What's the difference, then, between the priesthood and consecrating your life to Christ (each group has dedicated their lives to Christ)? The difference is that the priesthood is part of the formal hierarchy, or ruling body, of the Church. The priests are the official leaders of the Church, from your local priest to the pope, from your local parish to the Vatican. Religious brothers and sisters are not part of the hierarchy of the Church, but they do have a distinctive mission:

> *From the beginning of the Church, there have been men and women who have chosen to live in a radical witness to Christ by imitating him as closely as possible in his poverty, chastity, and obedience...*
>
> *They enrich the Church not only by the radicalness of their embrace of the evangelical counsels, but also by the many apostolates (e.g., education and health care) by which they follow Christ in his compassion and care for others. -USCCA, page 135*

Through the dedication to their mission, religious brothers and sisters extend the work of the priesthood, and the work of Christ, even further.

As an outsider looking in, the Catholic Church can seem like a confusing hierarchy of individuals with some unique titles, but when we break it down to its simplest forms, it is not so difficult to understand. Like any large organization, there are a number of roles and responsibilities within the Church, but we can understand by their titles where they fit into the system. The ministerial priesthood, with the help of our religious brothers and sisters, helps to spread the Gospel throughout the world. They lead the Church, teach our local parishes, help the poor, and serve the needy. If we are the body of the Church, they are surely the backbone that holds us together.

Back to Dedication

Earlier in this chapter, I shared with you how my lack of dedication to my calling, my ministry, and my God caused me to lose focus on my purpose in life. Friends, if you learn nothing else from the priesthood, learn this: their dedication to God and their faith is unmatched. It is an example for us to follow. If I had even a small portion of that dedication ten years ago, my life would have turned out much differently. Instead of spending over a decade wandering the desert of my own unfaithfulness, I may have been able to accomplish many exciting things in the name of God. Now, I am barely getting started.

Our priests, bishops, and deacons, as well as our religious brothers and sisters, dedicate their entire lives to God. Many of them choose a life of poverty. They give up the worldly view of their appearance and choose to wear religious habits and garb. They choose to remain celibate (excluding currently married deacons, of course) for the rest of their lives. The sacrifices they make in order to have a deeper relationship with Christ are staggering. They are not forced into that lifestyle; they choose it freely. Anyone that cannot find inspiration in their examples is simply lost.

Not everyone is called to the priesthood or religious life, but that does not mean that we should have any less dedication to God. We can mirror the example set by our religious leaders in other aspects of our lives. In our careers, we can work each day as if we are working for the Lord. At home, we can lead our families, especially our children, on the path to holiness. In public, we can openly and freely share our faith and love of Christ. Our actions reflect our dedication. We may not be part of the ministerial priesthood, but we are still part of the common priesthood. As members of the common priesthood, we are called to do more than follow the example of others' dedication; we must be the example of dedication for those around us.

Our Path

Ten years ago, I never would have chosen to follow priests in long robes over a modern pastor in blue jeans, but today, I love and respect the men and women that enter the religious life. Their devotion to God is beyond admiration, and we can never thank them enough for the work that they do for the Church. I never expected my path to end up here; however, looking back, I can see how this is truly where I am meant to be. It saddens me that I may never have a flock of my own, per se, yet I am happy to follow the shepherds that God has appointed over me.

One day, I may choose to become a deacon - that is something that I am still discerning - but for the time being I am happy to fulfill the role that God has chosen for me within the Church. A special few are called to Holy Orders, but that does not put the burden entirely on them. We must work together with our deacons, priests, and bishops to continue evangelizing and spreading the Good News about our Lord. Each one of us has a path that God is asking us to follow, and I am more than happy to allow Him to lead the way.

Chapter 4
The Trinity: Central Mystery of Our Faith

The Most Important Question

Who is God? Honestly, I never spent a lot of time thinking about it, but in all reality, it may be one of the most important questions we will ever ask. Defining God in a few sentences, paragraphs, or chapters is an impossible task. Entire books have been written on the subject, and they still fall short of being able to define the true essence of our Creator. We hear terms like *all-knowing, all-powerful,* and *ever-present.* Understanding the true meaning behind those words is difficult enough without even beginning to comprehend how they apply to God. Nonetheless, I believe that we need to have a basic idea of who He is and what He means to us. How can we say that we believe in God if we don't even know what (or Who) we believe in? We may never fully grasp the depths of God until, hopefully, we meet Him one day in Heaven, but for now, we need to, at least, agree on what we do know. So who is God? Let's take a little time to find out.

Ignorance is Bliss

I have been a Christian for many years now, and I thought that I had a pretty solid understanding of God's identity. He is the Trinity - that's about all I knew. And truthfully, I didn't even really understand what *that* meant. Somewhere along the line, someone told me that God is the Father, Son, and Holy Spirit - all at the same time. Beyond that, I didn't honestly know much. I considered myself a well-studied, well-read Christian who had read piles of books on the Christian faith. I could tell you all about prophecy, the Rapture, and the end of the world, yet I still did not have a basic idea on one of the most fundamental aspects of our faith: the identity of God.

Looking back at my years of Sunday school, I don't remember much. Somehow, knowing and understanding the identity of God was beyond the comprehension of a 9 year-old with little interest in sitting in that church classroom. I was more interested in the girl sitting next to me than the God who created me. As an adult, born-again Christian, we spent most of our time talking about all of the marvelous blessings God would bring into our lives, the hope that He brings, and the changes He would make in us. Deep, theological discussions on the essence of God were not the subject of rousing Sunday morning sermons. Still, I thought little of it. Knowing and comprehending God Himself just didn't seem that important. I respected the Father, gave my life to the Son, and felt the Holy Spirit working in my life. Beyond that, there is little more that I needed to know.

It all boiled down to one thing: me. All I cared about was who God was *to me* and what He would do *for me*. How He made it happen was entirely up to Him. It was a very self-centered view on faith. When we look at faith from this point-of-view, we put the focus on ourselves instead of on God. As Christians, our whole existence is meant to worship the glory of God, but how can we do that if we spend all of our time looking into the mirror? I was lost. Caught up in the glory of my own reflection, I knew little about the wonders and majesty of our Lord and King. When I finally realized the depths of my own vanity, I decided to change my focus from my sinful self to the wonderful Creator.

Many Views, One God

For a long time, I assumed that Christians, in general, had reached a basic consensus on the identity of God. True, we cannot comprehend His power and glory, but we know who He is. We all believe in pretty much the same thing, right? Wrong. I was shocked to find out that there are many different views on God. Despite the fact that we all clearly identify ourselves as Christians, we cannot even agree on this one, fundamental topic. What is the Trinity? Do we believe in one God, or three? Is Jesus truly divine? Is the Holy Spirit truly God? Are the Father, Son, and Holy Spirit equal to each other? Was Jesus *created* at His conception? These seem like some of the most fundamental questions we will ever ask about our faith, and shamefully, we cannot all seem to agree.

I, like many other Christians, did not know how vastly different our views were on the identity of God. I knew that other denominations practiced their faith a little differently, but I assumed that we could agree on this to some degree anyway. Many of the more structured denominations have very clear definitions of God's identity, even if you have to do a bit of searching to find it. Many of the less structured denominations, including some of the non-denominational churches that I once belonged to, do not spend a lot of time defining this. If anything, they may generically say that they believe in the Trinity without going into a lot of detail. That is where I formed many of my views. I believed in the Trinity, but I knew little more than that.

Does it matter? Do we actually have to define God? God is still God either way. And as hard as we may try to define Him, we will never even come close, so why bother? Because understanding the basic essence of God defines who we are as Christians. Belief in the Trinity impacts many other aspects of our faith. Knowing that Christ is divine is essential to our beliefs. Accepting the Holy Spirit as God into our hearts has the power to change our lives. Yes, it matters. In fact, few things matter more. If you want to call yourself Christian, if you tell the world that you believe in God, shouldn't you know what you are claiming to believe in?

Doctrine of the Trinity

As I was going through the RCIA process to join the Catholic Church, I was introduced to new concepts about the Trinity. The Church had clearly defined many aspects about God that put to rest many of the questions I had about His identity. Understanding and comprehending some of these topics may not be easy for some, but it cleared up some of my confusion surrounding it. The teaching was not based on recent revelations of one man trying to read the Bible; it was based on doctrine that dated back hundreds of years - as formulated by some of the greatest theological minds the Church has ever known. Finally, I could believe in something that had some real merit to it.

The Church believes that understanding the Holy Trinity is an essential part of our spiritual journey. In fact, the *United States Catholic Catechism for Adults* states,

> *The mystery of the Holy Trinity is the central mystery of the Christian faith and life. God reveals himself as Father, Son, and Holy Spirit. -USCCA, page 52*

The central mystery of the Christian faith? That sounds important. The Church does not glaze over the identity of God, like some other denominations do, because it recognizes how serious this concept is to our faith. It is the central mystery - the foundation - of our faith. We may struggle to understand many other Catholic doctrines, but this one is crucial. If you spend any time trying to learn the Church's view on our faith, begin right here.

Did you notice how the Church referred to the Trinity as a mystery? I did. Why would they call it a mystery? Because the Church acknowledges how difficult a concept this can be, even for the greatest of minds. As hard as we may try to grasp the idea of the Holy Trinity, it is still beyond our comprehension. God is greater than we can put into words. As I said earlier, volumes have been written about the Trinity and the identity of God, yet it only scratches the surface of who He really is. Still, as the *United States Catholic Catechism for Adults* tells us, we can break it down to three primary concepts: the Trinity is One, there are three distinct Persons to the Trinity, and each Person relates to the others.

One God

When Christians speak of the Father, Son, and Holy Spirit, some may begin to think that we see them as three separate gods, but there is only one God. Again turning to the *United States Catholic Catechism for Adults*, we learn:

First, the Trinity is One. We do not speak of three gods but of one God. Each of the Persons is fully God. They are a unity of Persons in one divine nature. -USCCA, page 52

This is the foundation of Christianity. We are monotheistic ("*mono*" meaning *one*) - a faith that believes in one God, and one God alone. If we break from this basic idea, then we are denying one of the most basic concepts of our faith.

St. Patrick was said to have used three-leaf clovers to explain this concept to the people of Ireland. When looking at a three-leaf clover, or shamrock, you can see three distinct leaves, but it still is part of one shamrock. Each of these leaves obviously represented each of the three Persons of God (Father, Son, and Holy Spirit), while the shamrock as a whole represented God Himself. Three leaves, one plant. Most people can accept this design in a simple plant; however, many still struggle to grasp the concept of one God in the Trinity. If this tiny plant can be this complex, why can't the Creator of the world be just as complex (and even more so)?

The tiny shamrock shares its resources with each of its leaves. Water, light, and nutrients are shared by the interconnections between them. Similarly, the three Persons of God share in the same divine nature. The divinity of God is shared between all three equally. They exist together in harmony and balance. This goes back to the mystery of the Trinity. Will we ever fully comprehend how this works? No. It is beyond our comprehension. Nonetheless, we can still accept the basis of this idea as an undeniable truth.

Three Persons

Some may try to oversimplify God by saying that the Trinity is just three different ways of God presenting Himself to us, but this is incorrect. The Trinity is, indeed, three separate Persons. Already, you have seen how the Church refers to the Father, Son, and Holy Spirit as *Persons* of the one, true

God. Continuing from the *United States Catholic Catechism for Adults*:

> *Second, the Divine Persons are distinct from each other. Father, Son, and Spirit are not three appearances or modes of God, but three identifiable persons, each fully God in a way distinct from the others.* -USCCA, page 52

Looking back to St. Patrick's example of a shamrock, each leaf is distinct from the others; it is not one leaf manifested in three ways. Each leaf is slightly unique and different from the others.

Each Person of the Holy Trinity is unique and has a purpose. The Father created the world and created each one of us. The Son is our Redeemer who became man and came to save us. The Holy Spirit is God within us, guiding us from inside our very hearts and souls. Their various roles have specific purposes in our lives. Together, the three Persons help us to connect to God in separate ways and form the relationship that we have with Him.

The mystery of the Trinity is deepened with this knowledge. How can the Lord be one God *and* three Persons at the same time? Again, only He knows how this is possible. Our job is not to question how this is possible - only to be thankful for a God who loves us enough to connect with us in these different ways. He loves us like a father. He understands our pain and sorrow as a man. He comforts us from within. This should be the primary reason that we love Him in return. It is for this reason that the Church calls the Trinity the "central mystery of the Christian faith."

Relations to Each Other

The final concept to understand about the Trinity is how the Three Persons relate to each other. They do not work alone; they work in harmony together. They even help to define each other. Completing this section from *United States Catholic Catechism for Adults*, we read:

> *Third, the Divine Persons are in relation to each other. The distinction of each is understood only in reference to the others. The Father cannot be the Father without the Son, nor can the Son be the Son without the Father. The Holy Spirit is related to the Father and the Son who both send him forth.* -USCCA, page 53

A father cannot be called a father without a son. All sons have fathers. And the Holy Spirit is the Advocate sent by the other two. In this way, the three Persons, as we know them, are defined by who they are to each other.

In our final look at St. Patrick's use of the shamrock, we can recognize one, simple idea about it. Would a three-leaf clover be the same if it did not have three leaves? If it had two, we would call it a two-leaf clover. Likewise, if it had four, we would call it a four-leaf clover. The three leaves of a shamrock define it for what it is, and in the same way, the three Persons of God define the Trinity. Without all three Persons, the Trinity would obviously not be the Trinity.

We will never understand the full mystery of God, but the relations between the Persons of the Trinity help to solve at least one piece of the puzzle. In the Old Testament, God was simply referred to as God, Lord, or Yahweh, but in the New Testament, we learn about the Persons of God. Why? Because Jesus came down to be with us, and after He was gone, God sent us the Holy Spirit. Although they had existed since the beginning, mankind was meeting them for the first time. Now, we could define God for all three Persons - we could define the

Trinity. We were beginning to know God more completely than before.

The Creed

We began by asking the question, "who is God?" By looking at and examining the mystery of the Trinity, I think that we have a better understanding of who God really is. But why do we accept this view of the Trinity? We know that there are many opinions on God's identity, and how to define Him, but where does this one come from? From the Catholic Church - almost 1700 years ago!

Questions about God's identity are not new. The same questions we asked earlier have been asked for thousands of years. Back in the 4th century A.D., a council was formed in Nicaea to answer some of these questions, and from that meeting came the Nicene Creed, which reads:

I believe in one God,
the Father almighty,
maker of heaven and earth,
of all things visible and invisible.

I believe in one Lord Jesus Christ,
the Only Begotten Son of God,
born of the Father before all ages.
God from God, Light from Light,
true God from true God,
begotten, not made, consubstantial with the Father;
through him all things were made.
For us men and for our salvation
he came down from heaven,
and by the Holy Spirit was incarnate of the Virgin Mary,
and became man.

For our sake he was crucified under Pontius Pilate,
he suffered death and was buried,
and rose again on the third day
in accordance with the Scriptures.
He ascended into heaven
and is seated at the right hand of the Father.
He will come again in glory
to judge the living and the dead
and his kingdom will have no end.

I believe in the Holy Spirit, the Lord, the giver of life,
who proceeds from the Father and the Son,
who with the Father and the Son is adored and glorified,
who has spoken through the prophets.

I believe in one, holy, catholic, and apostolic Church.
I confess one baptism for the forgiveness of sins
and I look forward to the resurrection of the dead
and the life of the world to come. Amen.
-The Roman Missal

Personally, I believe in the Creed with all of my heart. I believe in the three Persons of God as mentioned in the Creed. I believe the Father creates us, the Son saves us, and the Holy Spirit comforts us. The Nicene Creed defines our relationship to God in a truly special way, and it is for that reason that it is still used today and is part of the sacred liturgy of the Church, prayed at every Sunday Mass and Holy Days of Obligation.

Knowing God

I spent well over a decade calling myself a Christian but never genuinely knowing God. Hypocritical, I know. I was on fire for my faith but could not answer the most basic question: "who is God?" Various churches that I attended weren't much help because, as I realize now, they might not have known themselves. This topic, one of the first areas I explored while becoming Catholic, showed me, without a doubt, that I was on the right path in heading toward the Catholic Church. This central mystery of the Christian faith has helped me to broaden my spiritual journey in ways that I had never experienced before.

If you want to be Christian, you have to know God. You have to understand the different aspects of the Trinity. True, some of it may be confusing, but that is why even the greatest religious scholars call it a mystery. We will never fully understand the depths of God or the beauty of the Trinity, but we can know God, in a very personal, intimate way like never before. Let the central mystery of our faith, and the inspiring words of the Nicene Creed, bring your spiritual life to new levels. God knows you, and He wants you to know Him.

Chapter 5
Mother of Christ, Mother of the Church

To Believe, or Not to Believe

Few things stir more debates between Catholics and non-Catholics than the different views of Mary's role in the Church. With many years as a Protestant, it has been one of my own personal conflicts with Catholicism. From the Protestant perspective, Mary was the mother of Christ, something not to be taken lightly; however, Protestants and other non-Catholics are very reserved in their veneration of Mary. They choose not to hold her, or anyone else for that matter, in reverence. The belief is simple: no one deserves our love and adoration except the Father, Son, and Holy Spirit. I have held tightly to this belief since the time that I first found faith in Christ. Catholics, on the other hand, place Mary in a truly special place in the Church. As the mother of Christ, they believe she deserves veneration, and they look to her for intercessory prayers on their behalf. These two views oppose each other greatly. Which one do you believe?

The Protestant View of Mary

The Protestant church, born during the Reformation, opposed many of the teachings of the Catholic Church. Those teachings are central to the belief system of many Lutherans,

Methodists, Baptists, and non-denominational Christians. Growing up in a Lutheran home and going through Lutheran confirmation, I was taught these beliefs at an early age. Like most people, it has been tough to overcome many of those beliefs that were deeply ingrained into me as a child. The thought of Mary holding such a high place in many Catholics' lives seemed against everything that I had been taught. Sure, she must have been special to some extent. For God to have chosen her as the vessel to bear His Son, she must have done something right, but it was *His* ability to perform that miracle that is worthy of praise. Mary herself was simply a great woman chosen to a special calling, nothing more.

When I would see Catholic shrines honoring the Blessed Virgin, I scoffed at them. I was reminded of old teachings that stated we should not worship statues and false idols. How is it that Catholics can worship these statues, pictures, and images of Mary? It seemed blasphemous, to say the least. Speaking with Catholic friends and family, this was always one of the first topics that would come up. I would use the laws from the Old Testament as proof that the practice was wrong. Despite my best efforts, they always remained steadfast in their beliefs. Regardless of what I said, they never wavered from their love of Mary. Instead, they held to what they had been taught. To me, it seemed like an outdated, stubborn point-of-view.

Another problem that I had with the Catholic view of Mary dealt with the so-called sightings of Mary. Around the world, people flocked to places that Mary was said to have appeared. I remember laughing at a story of Mary being seen in a piece of toast, or something of that nature. Would God approve of us worshipping a piece of toast? Yet, to many Catholics that had seen apparitions of Mary, it was a sign that Mary was here in our everyday lives. There was story after story of Mary appearing to people, bringing hope, love, and guidance. Without a doubt, they must be losing their minds, I thought, but I could not deny that the stories intrigued me. To these people, their experiences were intensely real. Often times, the stories talked of miraculous transformations in people's lives. Was there any truth to these stories?

The Search for Mary

To find the Catholic interpretation of how Mary intercedes on our behalf, I turned first to the *Catechism of the Catholic Church* and the *United States Catholic Catechism for Adults*. I knew, so I thought, what the Bible taught about Mary, so I decided it was beneficial to get the purely Catholic point-of-view. Based on how Mary is woven into the everyday lives of Catholics through prayer, the Rosary, and through their general reverence, I knew that there would be a great deal of information on the subject. I expected for there to be hundreds of pages outlining why a good Catholic holds Mary in such high reverence. My first look began in the *United States Catholic Catechism for Adults*. I found a few passages on the subject, but not as much as I expected. Convinced that this must be an abridged version of the *Catechism of the Catholic Church*, I decided to look there next. Once again, I found only a few passages on the subject matter. How could this be? I could not find hundreds of pages dealing with the importance of Mary! In fact, I could not even find *tens* of pages dealing with Mary. How, then, could Mary be considered so important to Catholics?

I read and reread many of the passages. I couldn't find anything on a deeper level that would help me to understand the Catholic teachings on the Virgin Mary's role in the Church. Frustrated, I thought that my search was over before it began.

As a budding, new Catholic, I could not find the answers that I was looking for. How could I explain my recent conversion to Catholicism if I could not even explain one of the most highly debated of subjects? It led to more questions than answers. What next? After struggling to find the answer myself, I realized that prayer might be the key to a better understanding of the subject.

Still feeling lost, the true importance of the Blessed Virgin Mary was beyond me. Prayer seemed to be my only option left. Expecting to spend weeks meditating on the subject, I turned to the Lord while sitting on my living room couch. Not expecting an answer, I asked Him for a better understanding of what it meant. *Why do Catholics constantly seek the Virgin Mary?* The answer came sooner than I thought. In my heart, I felt, "The answer is right there. Read it again." With the Catechism in hand, I reread a portion entitled, "Mary-Mother of Christ, Mother of the Church." As I read through that section (CCC 963-975), it began to make sense. For all of this time, I had been searching for some deeper explanation of the Catholic view of Mary in the Church; however, it was so much simpler than that. In fact, it was in the straightforward, right-to-the-point text that truly gave me the answer. Simply put, the Blessed Virgin is a model of virtue that we should all hope to attain. By the choices she made, and her unwavering faith, she was an excellent example to follow.

Our blindness is often self-inflicted. In my case, my own misinterpretations of Catholic views led me to some false assumptions. Expecting volumes of information in the Catechism about Mary, the lack of information led me to struggle. I wanted to find pages and pages of reasons why I should hold Mary in such high regard. Instead, I found simplicity. The Catholic Church did not need to include hundreds of reasons why we should venerate Mary; only one is needed: she is the Mother of Christ. It is that simple. Being the Mother of Christ speaks volumes about this woman. For God to have chosen Mary to be the mother of His Son, she must have held a special place in His heart already. With God, nothing is an accident. Before she was born, Mary was chosen to be Christ's Mother. The Catholic Church can see the beauty of this woman based on that one fact (among many others, of course). Being able to see her from that point-of-view has opened my eyes and changed the way I see her. She is Mary, the Mother of Christ, worthy of our admiration.

The Catechism repeatedly speaks of Mary's faith and steadfastness. She was challenged with one of the most difficult tasks that any man or woman could be asked to do, yet she did not hesitate. Her role in the Church is as a model of faith and purity. For so long I had seen Catholics "worshipping" Mary, but what I had actually seen was their deep, utmost admiration of her. For a long time, I had only seen what I wanted to see. Now, with a clearer picture of the truth, I could begin to admire her myself.

Unanswered Questions

For many people, a simple answer will not suffice; there are still so many issues that a non-Catholic would have with the *dogma* surrounding the issue of the Virgin Mary. Few would argue that Mary's life of faith and purity was a fantastic model to follow, but does that mean that she should be *worshiped* in the same way Christ is worshiped? Of course, no one should be honored and glorified in the same way as the Father, Son, and Holy Spirit. So, why do Catholics worship Mary in this way? They don't. The Catechism tells us:

The Church rightly honors "the Blessed Virgin with special devotion. From the ancient times the Blessed Virgin has

> *been honored with the title 'Mother of God,' to whose protection the faithful fly in all their dangers and needs... This very special devotion... differs essentially from the adoration which is given to the incarnate Word and equally to the Father and Holy Spirit, and greatly fosters this adoration."* –CCC, 971, quoting Lumen Gentium 66

This exact quote from the Catechism itself explains the true view of the Church. They clearly define a difference between the devotion given to Mary and the adoration of God. It is said that Mary is venerated, or admired, not worshiped. As a non-Catholic, I questioned this. Here, with this passage from the Catechism, the record is set straight. It is acknowledged and explained in a way that is clear-cut and straightforward. If a Catholic worships Mary (and some incorrectly may) then he is wrong. Instead, it is taught that one should admire Mary for what she has done, and that it is right to honor her for that. This alone puts one of the greatest misunderstandings of the Catholic Church to rest.

Undoubtedly, Mary is worthy of our veneration. Her story is an example of true faith and devotion; one that we must not overlook. Pope John Paul II wrote,

> *Her exceptional pilgrimage of faith represents a constant point of reference for the Church, for individuals and for communities, for peoples and nations, and, in a sense, for all humanity. It is indeed difficult to encompass and measure its range.* -"On the Blessed Virgin Mary in the life of the Pilgrim Church", 1987

In other words, Mary's faith was great enough to inspire the entire globe for generations. Mary was chosen, but she still had choices to make. Like us, Mary had the free will to make those choices on her own. When faced with one of the greatest challenges mankind has ever known, Mary responded with strength, grace, and a steadfast heart.

Called by God

In the Bible, Mary's story begins when she is visited by an angel. Gabriel, the Archangel, came to deliver a message to her. When he first appeared, Mary was startled by him.

> *Then the angel said to her, "Do not be afraid, Mary, for you have found favor with God. Behold, you will conceive in your womb and bear a son, and you shall name him Jesus. He will be great and will be called Son of the Most High, and the Lord God will give him the throne of David his father, and he will rule over the house of Jacob forever, and of his kingdom there will be no end." -Luke 1:30-33, NAB*

Of course, Mary wondered, as a virgin how could she conceive a son? The angel explained to her that she would conceive a son through the Holy Spirit. Truly, this was a test of Mary's will - and of her faith in God.

The story of Christ's conception is a testament to the Blessed Virgin. When faced with life's challenges, many of us fail to rise to the occasion. Time and time again, we are called by God to step out of our comfort zone and do something greater. Far too often, we choose to ignore His calling and continue on with our lives. Mary, on the other hand, faced adversity without fail. She faithfully chose to serve the Lord, no matter what it may cost. Her faith did not waiver, and her life was given freely. Mary's devotion to her Lord is an example for us to follow and proof that she is worthy of our admiration.

A Life of Devotion

Raising children can be one of the greatest joys that we will ever experience. Mary's joy was not in raising just any child, but the Son of God. Children may be one of our greatest joys, but they are also the source of some of our greatest worries. As a father, I *would* go to great lengths to protect my children. As the Mother of God, Mary *did* go to great lengths to protect her Son, and it didn't take long for the need to arise. When King Herod learned that the "King of the Jews" was born, he set out to destroy Jesus by killing every firstborn son. To escape the king, Joseph, Mary, and Jesus fled to Egypt until it was safe. Only years later, after the death of the king, could they return to their homeland.

Like any son, Jesus worried His Mother. Once while on a trip to Jerusalem for Passover, Jesus had accidentally been left behind. His parents thought that He was with relatives, but He was not with them. They headed back to Jerusalem to go find Him. When I was a kid, I can remember playing hide-and-go-seek in the clothes racks at the local department store. I can also remember how frantic my mother would get. Mary must have been a wreck. Her young Son had wandered off, and she could not find Him. Days went by, and there was no sign of Him.

After three days they found him in the temple, sitting in the midst of the teachers, listening to them and asking questions... When his parents saw him, they were astonished, and his mother said to him, "Son, why have you done this to us? Your father and I have been looking for you with great anxiety." And he said to them, "Why were you looking for me? Did you not know that I must be in my Father's house?" Luke 2:46-49, NAB

That reminds me of the same *wise* answers that I would give my mother. Like any parent, Mary faced many of the same worries and challenges that parents do today.

Despite her best efforts, Mary could not protect her Son forever. Years later, when Jesus began His ministry, Mary continued to support her Son, but His time was short. Once again, while in Jerusalem for Passover, Jesus needed His mother the most. Betrayed by Judas, Christ was sent to the cross. The agony must have overcome her. Parents never want to see their child suffer, especially in such a cruel way, but Mary stood by her Son to the very last anyway.

> *Standing by the cross of Jesus were his mother and his mother's sister, Mary the wife of Clopas, and Mary of Magdala. When Jesus saw his mother and the disciple there whom he loved, he said to his mother, "Woman, behold your son." Then he said to the disciple, "Behold, your mother." And from that hour the disciple took her into his home. -John 19:25-27, NAB*

Moments later, He was gone. Some of His last thoughts were of His mother, this woman who had cared for Him so deeply. She was there when His life began. Painfully, she was there when His life ended.

When the Lord asked Mary to raise His only Son, Mary accepted a life of grief. Her world was thrown upside down from the moment that Christ was born. It began with the flight to Egypt, running for their lives, and ended with her Son being tortured and crucified. In Christ, Mary was given the greatest gift the world has ever known. With Christ's death on the cross, she was given one of the greatest sorrows the world has ever known. Mary accepted God's will and continued to follow Him even after His death. She trusted fully in God's plan and accepted the death of her Son.

As a mother, Mary was an example to us, the Church, on how we should lead our lives. There are times that God will ask us to flee into the desert. At other times, we may be searching for Christ, but we need to look no further than the Father's house. Lastly, He may ask us to lose everything and be separated from the ones we love. No matter what trials we may face, we should look to Mary as an example of strength, grace, and beauty. She lived her life fully devoted to God's will. If we have only a sliver of Mary's faith, we are truly blessed.

Our Mother

Mary, the Mother of the Church, has been at the forefront of shaping Christianity since the beginning. She was, in fact, the first to believe in Christ and His mission. Many non-Catholics, as I used to be, do not hold the same beliefs about her. They accept that she is special because God chose her, nothing more. The Catholic Church takes a slightly different view from Protestant churches: we honor her life by recognizing that she had to choose God in return. The Catholic Church venerates Mary for the faith she showed when asked to follow God's will. We honor her for the love and patience she showed as a mother. Beyond all of that, when you search deeply for why the Catholic Church looks for her guidance, the answer is simple: she is the Mother of Christ. As the Mother of Christ, Mary is the model of Christian life, through her faith, devotion, and unbending trust in God's Will.

Chapter 6
The Communion of Saints

A Saint by Any Other Name

Saints are a regular part of society - thanks to the widespread reach of Catholic values and teachings in our culture. Cities are named after saints, such as St. Louis, St. Paul, San Francisco, and San Diego. Hospitals, churches, and even businesses are named after these heroes of the faith, but does it offer any special protection? Why are saints named *saints* in the first place? What sets them apart from other Christians in history? Catholics have always held saints in such high regard, and as someone just beginning to explore the faith, I wanted to know why. Sure, they were outstanding examples and models of faith, but did they truly deserve that much honor and respect?

Praying to Statues and Other Nonsense

Few images will give a young Protestant, like my younger self, more ammunition than the image of a Catholic kneeling before a statue. Such heresy! How could Catholics kneel and worship a block of stone, wood, or plaster? What did they expect to get from a statue or picture of someone who died hundreds of years ago? Fine. I can understand respecting the faithful lives that they once lived, but that does not mean that we should worship them! It was borderline idolatry. They were worshipping false gods, instead of the one, true God. Good Protestants, like myself, needed to help cure Catholics of this horrible disease.

In my many debates with Catholics, they claimed that they were not worshipping the saints - they were merely asking them to pray on their behalf. What's the point of that? If I needed to pray for something, I just went directly to God myself. Why did I need someone to pass the message along for me? God is available to all of us, and Jesus is our Mediator. To me, it seemed like a waste of time - and a prayer - to ask a saint to pray for me. What if the saints couldn't pray for us? Did God still hear our prayers? It seemed like too much of a risk, and it seemed much easier just to take my prayers directly to God myself.

A Reason to Quit

As I continued in the RCIA process to become Catholic, I was convinced that I would eventually come to that "a-ha!" moment that would tell me that I shouldn't move forward. I thought it might be something about the pope, Sacred Tradition, or the Virgin Mary, but if I could not find a reason to quit through one of those, I was sure that learning more about the Catholic view of saints would. It had to be idolatrous. There is no way that I could become Catholic if they were teaching heresy. I was looking for an excuse, and I was certain that this was the place to find it.

I felt God leading me to explore the Catholic Church more, but I was still hesitant. Early on in the process, I told myself that I would not make the decision to become Catholic until the very end: the day before my Confirmation. It was at that time when I had to begin choosing a saint for my

Confirmation name, so I had purposefully put off researching the saints until then. I was too busy trying to learn and pick apart other Catholic doctrine anyway. Saints would have to wait for another day.

By the time Lent came around, just before my Confirmation, I was so ingrained into the Catholic faith that I had forgotten my objections. At this point, I was excited to choose a saint until I was reminded of my earlier convictions. "Wait!" I thought, "What if I realize this is idolatry? Have I become just like the other Catholics?" With this thought now plaguing my mind, I knew that I had to start learning more about the saints before it was too late. Little did I know, God was about to confirm that saints really do have a place in our lives.

Feast Days

Before I could choose a saint, I had to learn more about them. A few minutes' drive from work, I found a chain bookstore that I could visit on my lunch hour. When I had time, I would browse through the handful of books on saints, trying to find one that fit me the most. I did not know much about the lives of the saints, so I was truly starting from the beginning. I didn't know St. Francis from St. Thomas Aquinas. If they were not a major character in the Bible itself, I probably didn't even know their names, so searching for a saint that somehow represented me proved more of a challenge than I had originally thought.

One day, while browsing through one of those books, I started reading about St. Ignatius of Loyola. As a military veteran, adult college student, aspiring writer, and someone passionate about spirituality, he seemed like a perfect fit. We had a lot in common, and I could identify with the struggles that he faced in life. Finding someone whose life paralleled mine opened my heart to the idea of having a saint as a friend and ally. At the time, I didn't know the reach or impact that he, and the Jesuit order he founded, would have on the face of the Church (and the world) today. He was just one saint in a book full of them. In the end, I chose Ignatius as my Confirmation name because of the parallel events in our lives

Weeks went by before I first learned about Catholic feast days. I learned that some Catholics choose to celebrate their saint's feast day instead of their own birthday. This was a new concept to me. My first reaction was to look up St. Ignatius's feast day. What day would I be celebrating? If it was a fun date, I might consider celebrating it myself. Well, when I looked it up, the answer shocked me: St. Ignatius's feast day *is* my birthday. Chance? Coincidence? Possibly. Or was it God confirming to me the role of saints in our lives? Was it God showing me, despite my stubbornness, that we could open our hearts to the saints and allow them to be our allies? Believe what you want, but it helped me realize that the saints are there for each one of us, constantly offering up their prayers on our behalf.

The Communion of Saints

As a Protestant, non-denominational Christian, I did not believe in the Catholic idea of individually recognized saints; instead, I believed that members of Christ's Church, both past and present, were members of the communion of saints. The term *saint*, in this sense, simply means the holy, sanctified members of the Church, both on earth and in heaven. What I didn't realize is that Catholics believe in the communion of saints, as well. Quoting directly from the Catechism of the Catholic Church, "The communion of saints *is* the Church" (CCC, 946, emphasis added). This made me realize, at least in one respect, that we have more in common than I originally thought.

Both Catholics and Protestants alike, as well as other denominations (such as Eastern Orthodox), have similar views on the communion of saints. How do we differ then? It seems that the primary difference is that Catholics choose to recognize and honor certain Christian brothers and sisters that are known to have led faithful lives. There is now a formal process where the Church evaluates a person for sainthood. Basically, they try to determine if there is evidence of the person living a holy life, and even evidence of their intercession for us from heaven - proof that they are truly a saint.

We spend a lot of time arguing the differences between our different denominations, but in the case of the saints, we often share similar viewpoints. We can all agree that the communion of saints exists, both in heaven and on earth. The communion of saints is the collection of God's people, His Church. Let's focus, then, on that commonality between us. We are not that different. The Catholic Church, steeped in rich tradition, chooses to recognize some of those saints, but there is nothing heretical about that. If we can all agree that saints exist, what are we actually arguing about?

Honoring Our Heroes

Is there anything wrong with recognizing someone who lived a heroic life? Can we not recognize George Washington and Abraham Lincoln as great Americans? Can we not recognize the valor of the soldiers, sailors, and airmen that gave their lives for our country? Why, then, can we not recognize the work of the saints, such as St. Paul, St. Peter, St. Francis of Assisi, and St. Ignatius of Loyola? Why can't we recognize the sacrifices made by the martyrs who gave up their lives in the name of Christ? Just as we recognize our great American heroes, we can also recognize the many Christian heroes that have come before us.

Do you remember a loved one? A parent? Grandparent? Aunt, uncle, brother, sister, friend? Living or not, the people in our lives, both past and present, can be an inspiration to us. Remembering and honoring them does not mean that we worship them; it simply means that they are an everyday hero to us. In my life, my parents are one of many role models. My dad is quiet but strong, and we share a similar personality. My mom has overcome years worth of hard times that started at childhood, yet she always endured. Even after they are gone, I will remember the example they set for me. May no one fault me for that.

When I look at the life of St. Ignatius, he inspires me by his faith. Was he sinless? No. He was a sinner, just like you and me. But his life serves as an example for me to follow. I can read his *Spiritual Exercises*, learn how he overcame obstacles, and know that if he can overcome life's troubles, so can I. Like the American heroes who came before me, and my parents who set such a good example, St. Ignatius is someone that I can use to inspire myself in the most difficult situations. I may not know him personally, but I can follow the path he set before me.

Statues and Images

Have you ever visited the Washington Monument? The Lincoln Memorial? Mount Rushmore? A war memorial? If we can carve the faces of our American leaders into the side of a mountain, why can't we carve the image of a saint into a statue? If we can hang the picture of George Washington in our classrooms, why can't we hang a picture of St. Francis in our homes? It makes little sense to honor our country's heroes, but not our heroes of the faith. Our military veterans are model examples of what it means to be an American, and likewise, the saints are model examples of what it means to be a Catholic and Christian. In my home and office, you might not find a picture of Abraham Lincoln, but you will find images that honor the lives of the saints.

Undoubtedly, we all have (or will) lose someone close to us. When they pass, should we remove every sign of them from our homes? Should we take down their pictures from the wall and remove them from our albums? Of course not. These images are there to remind us of the wonderful lives they lived and the impact they had on us. They may be gone, but they are not forgotten. Their memory lives on in our hearts, and these images are gentle reminders of it.

Statues and images of the saints are also gentle reminders to us. It is not the image or statue itself that we honor, but the person it represents. Still, this does not mean that we are worshipping that person, but following their path to God:

> *The faithful do not worship pictures and statues; they venerate or honor the Virgin Mary and the saints and worship and adore only God. The veneration of Mary and the saints ultimately leads to God. -USCCA, page 297*

The saints led lives that brought them to Heaven, which should also be our ultimate goal. By following their example, and using pictures and statues as a reminder, we can also grow closer to God and find our way to eternal life. The images themselves have no special power, but our faith in Christ surely does.

Prayers of the Saints

Some may disagree with Catholics asking for the prayers of a saint. I once did. They believe in praying to God directly, and not through the intercession of the Blessed Virgin Mary or the saints. Of course, there is nothing wrong with praying to God directly; it is a blessing that each one of us has. Personally, I still pray to God on a daily basis. At the same time, I have also learned to ask for the prayers and intercessions of the saints, and it has had some amazing results. My first experience with this actually came years before I became Catholic.

After going through some pretty rough times, my life was left in shambles. My mistakes had led me to a life where some might have lost hope. I refused to give up, but I also felt overwhelmed by the mountain that I had to climb. My sister, herself a devoted Catholic, recognized my struggles and gave me a prayer card for St. Jude, the Patron Saint of Lost Causes. That in itself should be evidence of how far my life had spun out of control. I didn't believe in praying to saints. I didn't know if it would do any good. But I did know that it couldn't hurt, so I said the prayer anyway. Days turned into weeks, weeks into months, months into years. I can't tell you that my life turned around over night, but it did turn around. And I truly believe that St. Jude was praying for me, helping me to carry on through my struggles.

Still not convinced? When you are facing a time of struggle, have you ever asked someone to pray for you? Have you prayed for sick relatives, friends going through financial troubles, or loved ones dealing with emotional issues? We, the communion of saints on earth, pray for each other all the time, and we can ask the communion of saints in heaven to do the same. By asking the saints to pray on our behalf, we are inviting a team of prayer warriors to join us by our side. When we join our prayers with the saints, imagine the power that it can have! The *United States Catholic Catechism for Adults* tells us:

> *Here on earth we routinely ask others for prayers. Instinctively, we turn to holy people for their prayers because they seem nearer to God. Why would we stop asking saints for their prayers after they die? If we believe they are in heaven, would not their prayers be even more effective?* -USCCA, page147

The saints can actually help our prayers with their unique place in God's heart. Remember the last time that you applied for a job? They often ask for references, right? You could stand on your own merit, offering no references at all, or you could give a list of past coworkers to vouch on your behalf, which is far better than doing it on your own. As good as these references may be, it is even better to have a reference at the company you're applying to, especially if he or she holds a position of authority. With the right references, you have a better chance of getting the job. Similarly, when you ask the saints in heaven to pray on your behalf, it's like having the highest of references for your prayers. For that reason, Catholics all over the world turn to the saints in their prayers, asking for their help and intercession.

Saints: Heroes and Friends

Saints can serve as both our heroes and role models, as well as our friends who pray for us. For a long time, I found that difficult to understand. I was convinced that the topic of saints would be the final straw, and I would turn my back on Catholicism forever. But the more I learned, the more I fell in love with the saints. Now, I have a picture of St. Ignatius across from my desk, a constant reminder to live a saintly life. I ask for the prayers of St. Francis to help me steadfastly continue my mission. The saints have woven their way into my existence, and I am glad that they are there. Imagine the day when we finally greet each other in heaven. When we, the communion of saints, finally all get together, it may be the first time we meet, but it will feel more like a family reunion.

The saints can be an essential part of our faith if we so choose. Some will embrace the saints with all of their heart and reap the benefits that come with it. Others may choose not to, and that's okay too. For me, it has been a gradual process as the saints have made their presence more clearly known each day. I have always believed in the communion of saints but doubted their impact or ability to help. Now, with real experience of their intercession on my life, I am glad to call them my allies, my friends, my brothers and sisters in Christ.

Chapter 7
More Than Bread and Wine

Practicing Our Faith

Simply saying that we believe in God is not really enough. How many times have you heard people say that they believe in God without seeing it in their actions? Unfortunately, this is all too common. Practicing our faith is a crucial part of being a Christian, and for Catholics, this begins with Holy Communion, the Eucharist. Holy Communion means different things to different people, especially as we look at various Christian denominations. Some believe that it is simply a way to honor and remember Christ's sacrifice on the cross - nothing more. Others see it as a symbol of Christ's love that can have a lasting impact on our lives. But for Catholics, it means so much more. Catholics believe in *transubstantiation*, or the changing of the substance of the bread and wine into Christ's body and blood. That was a difficult concept to grasp, especially for a non-denominational Christian like myself. Was there any truth to the Catholic view on the Eucharist?

First Communion

Communion was nothing new to me. Growing up in a Lutheran home, it was a semi-regular part of my spiritual life as a child. Honestly, at the time, I did not fully understand what it meant, the Lutheran point-of-view, or why we were doing it. I knew that it somehow represented Jesus dying for us on the cross, but I never thought about it much more than that. All I truly remember was how awful wine tasted. I am still not a fan of it to this day. I avoided it as much as possible, which wasn't difficult because our family didn't attend church that regularly. When we did go, I remember avoiding communion any way I could.

At school, friends were telling stories about their First Communion. They were Catholic kids that had taken communion for the first time. Why was it such a big deal? I remember feeling sorry for how often those friends had to attend church. It seemed like they were going multiple times a week just to complete all of the Catholic requirements. I felt lucky to avoid all of that. Sure, I went about once a week for an hour or so, but that was manageable. I knew that in a few short years, I would be confirmed, and I could leave it all behind me. Communion was a part of that. It wasn't a big deal. We didn't have a special party for it; it was just something that we did.

Merely a Symbol

Years later, long after my confirmation as a Lutheran, I became a *born again* Christian. After years of drifting spiritually, including some time as a self-avowed atheist, I finally saw the need for Christ in my life. Returning to the Christian life brought back a lot of those childhood memories, including Communion. I didn't return to my old Lutheran church; it was too old-fashioned for my tastes. Instead, I found a home at the local mega-church, a non-denominational powerhouse where you could have a cup of coffee in the cafe while watching the sermon from a large projection screen.

There were bright lights and modern music - everything a twenty-something with a newfound faith could ever need.

Once a month, they held a special service for communion during the week. For those that still enjoyed this practice from other churches and denominations, they could come take part in this symbolic ritual of Christ's death on the cross. It wasn't mandatory. It didn't offer any special graces. It was simply a time to come and reflect on Jesus' sacrifice. Instead of wine, they had a non-alcoholic, grape juice alternative that was well-suited to my tastes. Communion was not something that I attended regularly, but it was a nice sentiment from time to time. Somehow, I felt that I was holding onto a small part of my family's tradition, at least in some small way.

Catholics Believe What?

When I first started going to RCIA, I also began going to Mass regularly with my new girlfriend (who I'm lucky to call my wife). I was shocked to find out that I couldn't take communion with the rest of the people there. Somehow, because I was not Catholic yet, I did not have permission to take the Eucharist. This was upsetting. I had grown up in a Christian home, and I had been an on-fire, strong Christian for well over a decade already. Who were they to tell me that I was not spiritually prepared to take the Eucharist? This alone was almost reason enough to not come back again.

It was embarrassing to step aside while the "real Catholics" marched their way up to the front. My faith was real, probably more real than many of those who attended each week out of some sense of duty. I needed to find out why I wasn't allowed. With a little research on the Internet, and a few questions to Catholics I knew, I found out that it boiled down to primarily one thing: *transubstantiation.* "*Trans-sub-stancha-what?*" I asked. Exactly. I could not take Holy Communion in the Catholic Church because I did not understand it the way they did. The Eucharist is a Sacrament, an important part of the Catholic faith, and I could not participate until I fully understood and believed it.

So what is transubstantiation? As I read online, Catholics believe that the substance of the bread and wine actually transform into the real body and blood of Jesus Christ. Catholics believe what? No, no, no, no. It's just a symbol, right? It's not *actually* the body and blood of Christ, is it? Is that what they actually believe?

I was amazed, dumbfounded, and confused. Could I seriously accept that the body and blood of Christ are really present up on that altar? Could I accept that I would be taking God into my body? I had never known that this is what Catholics believed. In the past, I had just assumed that everybody saw it as a mere ritual - a symbol of our faith. This, I realized, could be a life-changing concept. Either it would turn me away from the Catholic Church forever, or my world was just opened up to an amazing truth. It could only be one or the other, not both. If Catholics had figured out how to make Jesus present in a real, tangible way, I had to know more.

John 6

After learning about the basic idea of transubstantiation, I didn't run home to find out more right away. Truthfully, it was more than I could handle at the time. I was still doing my best to absorb a host of other Catholic doctrines, and this one seemed way too complicated. Finally, it began to bother me as I stood by each week at Mass, so I began to do a little research. Was this just another Catholic dogma?

Where was the Biblical proof for this one? I don't remember reading anything about that in the past, so what proof would I find for this? Turns out, all I had to do was read John 6.

At the beginning of John 6, we read the story of Jesus feeding a large crowd with just two fish and five loaves of bread. His miracles had drawn large crowds, and it took even greater miracles to feed them all. That night, Jesus took off with His disciples across the sea, and when the crowds realized He was gone, they followed. Jesus was actually upset by this, not because they wanted to see Him, but because they had simply come to get more to eat. They cared more about their physical hunger than their spiritual hunger. Jesus responded:

> *"Our ancestors ate manna in the desert, as it is written:*
> *'He gave them bread from heaven to eat.'"*
> *So Jesus said to them, "Amen, amen, I say to you, it was not Moses who gave the bread from heaven; my Father gives you the true bread from heaven. For the bread of God is that which comes down from heaven and gives life to the world." -John 6:31-33, NAB*

Simple enough. The bread we eat, both physically and spiritually, is a gift from God. In my view of communion as a symbol, I can understand that, but later in the chapter, the story continues:

> *"I am the bread of life. Your ancestors ate the manna in the desert, but they died; this is the bread that comes down from heaven so that one may eat it and not die. I am the living bread that came down from heaven; whoever eats this bread will live forever; and the bread that I will give is my flesh for the life of the world."*

> *The Jews quarreled among themselves, saying, "How can this man give us [his] flesh to eat?" Jesus said to them, "Amen, amen, I say to you, unless you eat the flesh of the Son of Man and drink his blood, you do not have life within you. Whoever eats my flesh and drinks my blood has eternal life, and I will raise him on the last day. For my flesh is true food, and my blood is true drink. Whoever eats my flesh and drinks my blood remains in me and I in him. Just as the living Father sent me and I have life because of the Father, so also the one who feeds on me will have life because of me. This is the bread that came down from heaven. Unlike your ancestors who ate and still died, whoever eats this bread will live forever." -John 6:48-58, NAB*

Did Jesus really say that? Did He actually say that His flesh is true food and His blood true drink? I was just as confused as the Jews in this story were.

Okay, so based on this verse, Jesus genuinely wants us to take part in Holy Communion, but like many other Protestants, I still believed that Jesus was speaking symbolically. The Last Supper had not happened yet, so the crowd simply misunderstood what He was teaching. In time, they would understand. But then, I kept reading, and it was the next few verses that opened my eyes:

> *Then many of his disciples who were listening said, "This saying is hard; who can accept it?" Since Jesus knew that his disciples were murmuring about this, he said to them, "Does this shock you? What if you were to see the Son of Man ascending to where he was before? It is the spirit that gives life, while the flesh is of no avail. The words I have spoken to you are spirit and life. But there are some of*

you who do not believe." Jesus knew from the beginning the ones who would not believe and the one who would betray him. And he said, "For this reason I have told you that no one can come to me unless it is granted him by my Father."

As a result of this, many [of] his disciples returned to their former way of life and no longer accompanied him. Jesus then said to the Twelve, "Do you also want to leave?" Simon Peter answered him, "Master, to whom shall we go? You have the words of eternal life. We have come to believe and are convinced that you are the Holy One of God." - John 6:60-69, NAB

Many of Jesus' disciples left. Did He stop them? Did He try to re-phrase what He had said? Did He try to help them understand that He was just speaking symbolically? No.

Jesus was not speaking symbolically about the Eucharist. He truly meant that they would have to eat His flesh and drink His blood. Even when the crowd was beginning to leave, He did not try to stop them because He knew that they would have a hard time accepting this as true, just as many struggle to accept this truth today. Who stood by Him? St. Peter and the Apostles. As usual, St. Peter stands up as the early leader of the Church and proclaims that they will stand by His side. They may have a difficult time grasping what He is teaching, but they believe that what Jesus is saying is true. This truth, as strange as it may seem to those outside the Church, is still guarded today by the Pope and his bishops, the successors of St. Peter and the apostles. They are convinced, just as St. Peter was, that Jesus is the Holy One of God.

Newfound Respect

The story of John 6 changed me, and I had a newfound respect for the Eucharist. Instead of being upset about waiting to receive the Eucharist, I waited in joyful expectation of the first time that I would receive the body and blood of our Lord when I was formally received into the Church. While many Catholics had forgotten the true meaning of Holy Communion, I understood the power and grace that came from it. Months later, when I was finally confirmed at the Easter Vigil, I can remember the excitement I felt when our parish priest offered me the Blessed Sacrament for the first time. Wonderful. Simply wonderful.

There was one side effect to my newfound respect: frustration. Frustration for those who walked out the door the moment they received Communion. Frustration for those who walked up to the altar with little reverence for what was about to happen. Frustration for those who only wanted to receive Jesus twice a year at Christmas and Easter. It is a shame to see this happening in our Church, but we can do something about it - we need to teach and remind our brothers and sisters about the amazing grace that comes to us in the Blessed Sacrament. I was once ignorant to the beauty of the Eucharist. Who am I to judge anyone else? We should not judge anyone; instead, let's re-catechize them on the glorious miracle that happens at the altar.

The Eucharist in Our Daily Lives

This chapter began by discussing the importance of practicing our faith. It is not enough to simply say that we are Catholic; we need to participate in the Catholic faith - especially the sacraments. The best way to bring the sacraments into our daily lives is the Blessed Sacrament, the Eucharist.

Now that we understand its importance (because of Christ's real presence through transubstantiation), we need to find ways to focus our spiritual lives on this sacrament. Fortunately, the Church has a number of ways that we can incorporate it into our personal faith.

The first, and most obvious, way is by attending Mass weekly (or daily if you are blessed to have the time). At Mass, we have the opportunity to receive the Blessed Sacrament with our fellow Catholics. We spend a great deal of time in worship and prayer leading up to the actual Communion Rite. Each step leading up to this moment is meant to prepare our heart for receiving Christ. In the Liturgy of the Word, we are fed by Sacred Scripture with selected readings for the week and a homily. In the Liturgy of the Eucharist, the altar is prepared, and we say a series of prayers that reflect old traditions. The Mass culminates in our actual reception of the Eucharist, and with our hearts and minds in the right place, this is a particularly special moment.

Another way to enjoy this Sacrament is through adoration. We show adoration to God through the Eucharist as we genuflect before entering the pew. We also show adoration as we bow when approaching the altar. Some parishes, like my own, are lucky enough to have an adoration chapel, a place where the Blessed Sacrament is placed in a monstrance for us to view, pray before, and adore. Spending time in adoration of the consecrated host is a fantastic way to grow even closer to God in our daily lives. If you cannot attend Mass daily, this is an excellent way to fill the time between Sundays. Go there to say a rosary, read from your Bible, or just reflect on the inner stirrings of your heart.

Finally, you can also become an Extraordinary Minister of Holy Communion. Some may incorrectly say *Eucharistic Minister*, but in actuality, only bishops, priests, and deacons are considered ordinary ministers of the sacrament. Either way, an extraordinary minister can help distribute the Eucharist to the congregation, and when someone is too sick or ill to come to church for the Eucharist, he or she can actually be sent to administer it at their home or a hospital. Few things could be more honorable than bringing the Blessed Sacrament to someone who could not receive it otherwise. Think of the grace that you are bringing to that person's life. Amazing.

I encourage you to find ways to make this Sacrament a central part of your faith. Not only is it evidence of your practical spirituality, but it will bring graces beyond measure. In the Eucharist, we receive the true body and true blood of our Lord, Jesus Christ, and we should want to do everything we can to draw closer to Him in this way. The Church actually requires that we go to Mass on a weekly basis, but we should not see it as simply a requirement. It is a blessing each week that helps keep us grounded in our faith and recharged for the week to come.

The Eucharistic Life

The Eucharist. The Blessed Sacrament. Holy Communion. The true body and true blood of our Lord. For a long time, I understood the bread and wine to be mere symbols of our faith, a representation of Christ's work on the cross. I participated out of honor and respect for our Lord, yet expected nothing in return. Now with a better understanding of Christ's words in John 6, I know beyond the shadow of a doubt that I am receiving Christ's body and blood as the substance of the bread and wine is transformed through transubstantiation. Now I am excited to receive the graces that come from the Eucharist each week, if not more often than that.

I have been participating in Communion since I was a child, but now, as a Catholic, I can say that I take part in *Holy* Communion, the Eucharist. It was challenging to accept the Church's doctrine on the sacrament, but once I did, I was amazed at the graces that flowed from it. We must make the Blessed Sacrament a cornerstone of our faith, the most important part of each week. We can go to Mass, spend time in adoration, and become an extraordinary minister. The Eucharist can impact us in ways that we never expected. Before my confirmation, I was frustrated that I had to wait to receive the Eucharist, but now I see that it was entirely worth the wait.

Chapter 8
Reconciled

A Society in Need of Forgiveness

One look at modern society will tell you that sin is a serious problem. Greed, lust, and vanity are not only accepted, but embraced as a way of reaching one's *full potential*. With the glorification of sex, violence, and debauchery in modern movies, television, music, and books, it becomes even more difficult to resist the temptations that lead us to sin. Be that as it may, this does not give us the freedom to live a sinful life without consequences. Our actions will eventually catch up with us - and with all of society. Before the effects of our sins overcome us like a tidal wave, it is time that we repent from our ways and turn back to God. Society is in desperate need of forgiveness, and we can find the absolution we need through Christ. For many years as a devout Christian, I accepted the forgiveness offered to us on the cross, but as a Catholic convert, I was told that there was one more step in the process: the Sacrament of Penance, or Confession. But did I need to confess my sins to another man to find absolution? Did I have the courage to admit my mistakes openly? I am not alone. A large part of society is obviously dealing with these same obstacles.

When Good is Not Good Enough

You've no doubt heard these words before, "I am a good person - good enough to go to heaven." Really? Do people actually think that highly of themselves? Are we ever good enough to get to heaven? I thought so. My Lutheran childhood had little effect on me as a teenager, but even so, I was still a good kid. I didn't smoke, do drugs, or drink alcohol. My grades were slightly above average. Overall my life was about being just good enough to get by, maybe a little more, but there was nothing that was necessarily *great* about me. With the potential to do awesome things with my life, I squandered my teen years by only putting in the minimum effort needed. Would that same amount of effort guarantee me a spot in heaven? Does God reward us for doing the bare minimum?

Life soon led me to some dark places. My laziness caught up with me, and the consequences were more than I could handle. Depression quickly set in. It felt like being at the bottom of a well, staring back up at the sky, unable to climb back out again. There seemed to be no hope for my life anymore until, one day, I first saw the light of Christ. I can still remember the burdens of my past being lifted off my shoulders. For the first time, I realized how much my sins and past mistakes were weighing me down, not allowing me to move forward with my life. What an incredible feeling! As a *born again* Christian, I said a simple prayer, and my sins were forgiven. That was it. It was no longer about being good enough to get to heaven. I didn't have to be - I had Jesus on my side. Now, regardless of how good or bad I may be, Jesus had washed away my stains. Of course, I still tried my best to be a better person, but even if I failed it didn't seem to matter.

For the first few years after my conversion to Christianity, I rode the wave of my newfound faith. Sadly, it didn't last. Poor choices began to cool down the fire within me. Years later when I started learning more about Catholicism, I realized that I was doing it again. My faith had grown complacent. Prayer only came in times of greatest need, I only attended church when it was convenient, and there was little about me in both my words and actions that would let anyone know that I was a Christian. In short, I was back to being just good enough, and according to the Catholic Church, being good is not good enough - especially without going to Confession. My sins, primarily my apathy, had separated me from God once again.

Can Another Man Forgive Me?

Confession was a new concept to me. Sure, I had seen it in the movies - the hero goes into the confessional to tell the priest his sins before he or she went off to save the world from utter destruction. Real life Confession is nothing like that, of course, but it didn't make me believe or understand it any more. Why did I have to ask a priest for forgiveness? I thought that only God could forgive us. It was Jesus' death on the cross that brought us salvation, not a man sitting in a box. I understood the Biblical concepts behind the Eucharist, Baptism, and the vows of marriage, but understanding Confession was difficult. It went against everything I had learned for years as a Protestant. When I became born again, I turned my life over to Christ, and He gave me forgiveness in return. I saw little need for Confession, but if I wanted to become Catholic, I knew that it was a road that I would someday have to cross.

My analytical mind could spend hours defending myself and talking my way out of the confessional. I had every excuse. In the end, though, it was fear more than anything. How embarrassing would it be to tell my deepest secrets to a man I hardly knew? How could I openly admit each and every one of the mistakes that I had made over a lifetime? The shame was more than I could handle. Deep-rooted guilt overcame me. Somehow, I was able to dodge the confessional for quite a long time, yet I could never escape the Holy Spirit gently tugging at my heart, telling me that I desperately needed this. Scared and nervous, I finally decided that it was time to go, but it happened sooner than I expected.

Spiritual Retreat

A few friends had talked me into going to a spiritual retreat. By this time, my faith was much stronger than it was before, I was a relatively new Catholic, and I was continually learning more and more about the Catholic faith. Attending a retreat aimed at bringing people back to the faith seemed a few steps behind where I was; even so, I went anyway. Maybe a weekend focused on God would be a good thing - a time to break away from the noise of the world and turn my attention completely to Him. I was slightly nervous about going, I didn't know what to expect, but I was also looking forward to a weekend with few worldly obligations.

The retreat was going well. It was Christian Spirituality 101, nothing new to a seasoned, formerly born again Christian, but I still enjoyed the time I had with others. As the retreat continued, they told us that we would have the opportunity to go to Confession near the end of the retreat. My heart sank. I had never gone before! Now, I had to go for the very first time with a group of people waiting in line behind me. I should have gone as part of the RCIA process, but somehow that didn't happen. I didn't know what to do, or what to say. My mind was racing. I did the only thing that a professional nerd, like myself, would do: searched the Internet. But finding out the process of the Sacrament was much different from actually being there. What should I do? Part of me contemplated not going back to the final day of the retreat just because of it. I had a decision to make - and soon!

The next day, I woke up extremely nervous. In a few short hours, I would be face-to-face, or face-to-curtain-to-face, with a priest, telling my whole life story to him. When the time came, I stood in line impatiently. My palms were sweating. My face was flush. From head to toe, I could feel my nerves on edge. As I stepped into the confessional, I bluntly told the priest, "I don't know what I'm doing!" The very understanding man on the other side of the curtain helped me through the entire process. Tears rolled down my face. My heart began to feel extremely heavy, but then, as I told more and more about myself, it began to feel lighter. By the end, I felt a sense of peace and calm. Nothing magical happened. I didn't begin walking on water or speaking in tongues; I simply felt relieved, comforted, accepted, loved. Confessing my sins was a more spiritually gratifying experience than I had ever imagined.

Acknowledging Our Sin

Before we get into the process of the Sacrament of Confession, we need to understand why we need to go in the first place: because we are sinners. If we cannot admit that we have sinned, then Confession will do us little good. Few Christians would deny that they are sinners. We are taught, in fact, that we are *all* sinners. Mistakes will happen. Try as we may, we will fall short of living the life that God wants us to live. If we can all agree on that, then we simply need to admit to ourselves which sins made us sinners in the first place. Be honest with yourself. Do you know your sins? Can you look at your own life and recognize the mistakes you've made? You may not recognize them all - that comes with spiritual maturity and growth - but we should all be able to recognize at least some sin in our lives.

If we can admit that we are sinners, and we can recognize our sins, why would anyone question the need for Confession? Well, in the *once saved - always saved* mindset, some believe that accepting Christ (being born again) saves us once and for all. I once believed that too. The mindset is that Jesus will speak on our behalf at our judgment, regardless of our sins and past mistakes, as long as we have accepted Christ. There is one problem with that theory: in the Gospel of St. Matthew, Jesus states:

> *"Everyone who acknowledges me before others I will acknowledge before my heavenly Father. But whoever denies me before others, I will deny before my heavenly Father." -Matthew 10:32-33, NAB*

In the Catholic Church's eye, when we commit the deadliest of sins, we are denying Christ, and when we deny Christ, He will deny us, as well. Until John Calvin came along, that was a belief shared among the entire Church, and it is still held by many Protestant denominations today.

Was the Sacrament of Penance and deadly sins purely dogma of the Church, or was it Biblical? It's Biblical. In the First Letter of St. John, we read:

If anyone sees his brother sinning, if the sin is not deadly, he should pray to God and he will give him life. This is only for those whose sin is not deadly. There is such a thing as deadly sin, about which I do not say that you should pray. All wrongdoing is sin, but there is sin that is not deadly. -1 John 5:16-17, NAB

Let's turn that around. St. John acknowledges that some sin is not deadly, but that also means that some sin *is* deadly and needs more than prayer. Deadly sin is clearly Biblical. Even for those who hold tightly to *sola scriptura* (the belief that all doctrine must come from the Bible alone), there is no denying that these sins cannot be simply prayed away. So we must acknowledge our sins, and also acknowledge that our deadly sins will lead us away from Christ.

Confessing to a Priest

During my years as a Protestant, I had read the Bible, especially the New Testament, multiple times. I was well-versed in Scripture, but somehow I had glazed over these verses. With a better understanding of the deadly sins that separated me from God, I wanted to find absolution, but did that mean that I had to go to a priest? Do priests really have the ability to offer us forgiveness? Or can I simply go to God in prayer and ask to be reconciled to Him? According to the verse from 1st John, we need more than that. We have separated ourselves from God; therefore, we need someone to help us reconcile with Him again. That is where our priests come in.

Two verses from the Bible (among many others) help to illuminate this better. First, we learn that the practice of confessing to one another was Biblical:

> *Therefore, confess your sins to one another and pray for one another, that you may be healed. The fervent prayer of a righteous person is very powerful. -James 5:16, NAB*

An earlier verse in this chapter mentions summoning the presbyters of the Church, or priests, to pray over the sick, so in this verse, we see that the prayer of a righteous person (a priest) can bring healing after confession, as well. Without a doubt, we can see that the early Christians confessed their sins to one another. This practice has continued for two thousand years in the Sacrament of Penance.

The second verse we need to look at highlights the power given to priests to absolve us of our sins. Shortly after His death and resurrection, Jesus appeared to His disciples in the upper room. When He did:

> *He breathed on them and said to them, "Receive the holy Spirit. Whose sins you forgive are forgiven them, and whose sins you retain are retained." -John 20:22-23, NAB*

Again, beyond any doubt, we read in Sacred Scripture the affirmation needed to believe in the Sacrament of Confession. Jesus gave the apostles the power and ability to forgive sins. Of course, the true power and forgiveness comes from Christ's saving work on the cross, but He delegates that power down to them in the upper room. If one is looking for Biblical evidence for this sacrament, they need look no further than this.

Regular Confession

Now that we understand the Biblical significance of Confession, how often should we go? Although, the real question should be, how long can we afford not to go? Our mortal, deadly sins separate us from God. We should not wait any longer than necessary to be reconciled to Him. The Church's *Code of Canon Law* requires that Catholics confess at least once a year, but we should go as soon as we realize that we are guilty of a deadly sin. If we ran to Confession every time we sinned venially though, there would be long lines outside of the confessional on a daily basis. Because this is not practical, many would recommend going about once a month on average, even if we have only venial sins to confess. This helps to keep us reconciled to God on a regular basis.

Some will see this as just another duty of being a Catholic, similar to weekly Mass. Over time, they get frustrated with all of the requirements and can begin to drift away because of it. To avoid that, we need to stay focused on the purpose of Confession and the positive effects it can have on our lives, just as we would with Mass and the Eucharist. Going to Confession regularly helps to keep our slate clean. Confessing becomes easier each time, and we have less to confess. Instead of waiting until our burdens are too heavy to carry anymore, we free ourselves from them while they are still manageable. Monthly Confession leads to a less stressful, happier life.

Truly Free from Sin

My life began in mediocrity, which continued long after I had become a Christian. I continually chose the path of barely above average. While this path seemed easier at the time, it eventually led me to a host of other problems. In my spiritual life, I struggled to maintain the intensity of my faith because it lacked a strong foundation. Looking back, I can see that the sins of my past still weighed me down, and my life would not be able to move forward until I truly found absolution. Fortunately, the Holy Spirit intervened and sent me on the right path during that retreat. If I hadn't stumbled my way into Confession, who knows where my life would be today. I found an inner peace that day, a peace beyond words.

Since becoming Catholic, a few things have surprised me about Confession. What didn't surprise me is that it is nothing like the movies. I was surprised at the Biblical basis of the Sacrament. I had read those passages many times, yet never picked up on their significance. I was also surprised at the weight of my sins. As a Christian for many years, I thought that I was free from my burdens - only to find out that I was still shackled by them. Primarily, though, I was surprised at the way my fear quickly subsided and peace washed over me. Stepping into the confessional for the first time (or the first time in a long time) can be extremely difficult, but once we are there, we might be amazed at how life-changing it can be.

The Sacrament of Penance should be an important part of our spiritual lives. We focus heavily on the Eucharist, reading Scripture, and daily prayer; meanwhile, we are slowly drifting away from God and sinking because of our sins. We cannot let the weight of our mistakes leave us at the bottom of the well. Christ has given us the blessing of forgiveness that can easily be found behind the curtain of a confessional. Our wonderful, loving priests are there to guide and comfort you, and I know that it is time never wasted.

Find the courage to attend Confession, whether it's the first time ever as a new Catholic or the first time in years. If you're not Catholic yet, you'll have to go through the RCIA process first (except in special circumstances), but once you go, you'll be planning when you'll go again.

Chapter 9
Becoming Catholic

Turning Point

The sum and purpose of this book leads us to this very topic: being fully received into the Catholic Church. Each chapter has detailed the questions and struggles that I faced while going through the Rite of Christian Initiation of Adults (RCIA). I have opened up my heart and soul to share with you the difficulties that I faced, so that you may find comfort in facing the same challenges. Along with my personal story I have summed up the basic teachings of the Church, similar to what is taught in many RCIA programs in a straightforward, easy-to-understand way. My hope is that these teachings will inspire you to begin the RCIA program at your local parish and encourage you to continue your journey. As someone new to the faith, you have reached a turning point: remain as you are, or continue on the path to becoming Catholic. May these pages, with the help of the Holy Spirit, move you ever closer to the beauty of the Catholic Church.

Confirmed Again

When I began looking into Catholicism seriously, I learned that I would have to go through RCIA, which includes Confirmation. On some level, it upset me. As a child, I had already been confirmed as a Lutheran. I had been taught the basics of the Christian faith since I was young, and this continued until my teenage years when I was finally confirmed into the Lutheran Church. Some of my earliest memories, both good and bad, are of that process. Waking up early on Sunday mornings to go to class was never something that I enjoyed. Sure, I woke up at 7 a.m. on Saturdays to watch a morning full of cartoons, but waking up at that same time to go to Sunday school was not as much fun. I can even remember giving my dad a hard time as he dropped me off with the other kindergarteners. I was a shy kid, and this immediately took me out of my comfort zone. My dad tried to ease our pain with regular Sunday morning trips to the donut shop, but it barely made up for the trouble. Those times at the donut shop are some of my fondest memories; my time at Sunday school is not.

As a young teenager, I started the Lutheran confirmation process. This meant going to church on Sundays *and* one night during the week. Now the classes that I struggled with were taking up two days each week instead of only one. If the choice had been up to me I would not have gone; I would have dropped out. But my parents, who rarely attended church themselves, decided that we needed to have at least some understanding of the faith. Once my siblings and I were confirmed, we could then make our own choices about how we practiced the faith. I couldn't wait to get the process over with, and as soon as I did my shadow never darkened the doorway of the church again. Other than weddings and funerals I saw little need for church in my life, so my attendance stopped there.

It is little wonder that the Catholic Church asks us to go through Confirmation again, even if we have already gone for another denomination. I remembered little of what I had learned over those many years except for a few minor details about Christianity. An even more significant factor was that faith never took hold in my life during that time. After almost ten years of being taught the Word of God as a child, I still didn't believe in Him. During my childhood I was agnostic at best, and as I grew older I was a self-avowed atheist for most of my high school years, relying more on science than religion. How could the Catholic Church accept that as proper catechesis (especially considering that many of our doctrines are different anyway)? Looking back, faith never took a foothold in my life, and as an adult, maybe RCIA would be the process that could finally make that happen.

Information Cards

If you have read other chapters in this book, then you already know that my journey to Catholicism did not begin the moment I left the Lutheran church. Shortly after I left high school, I became a "born again" Christian. The Holy Spirit had opened my heart to the richness and wonder of the Christian faith. So did I run back to the Lutheran church where I grew up? No. I still remembered how long and boring those services could be and I wanted something more exciting. Most of the born again Christians I had met attended one of the local mega churches, including the young woman that unknowingly led me to my conversion. When I did go to church I generally went there. I went off and on but was never a regular fixture there, not that anyone would notice among the thousands of people that attended each week.

Over the next several years, my life took me to a variety of places primarily because I had joined the military. It was during those years that I first found a church to call home, so I decided to become a member. What's the process of becoming a member at the average nondenominational church? Fill out an information card, drop it in the offering plate, and attend a 2-hour information session - that's it. As I moved around the country I filled out a number of those cards, and as I got bored with or disagreed with the church I was attending, I filled out even more. The process made it extremely easy to bounce from church to church, holding no real affiliation or loyalty to any of them. Like many newcomers, with a lack of teaching for new members except for the weekly sermon, I found it difficult to plant roots in the faith. Once the initial excitement of conversion wears off, I was unsure of what to do next. Eventually, I simply drifted away.

Years later, finally back in my hometown outside of Chicago I took my first steps toward Catholicism. Imagine my surprise when I first contacted the local Catholic parish, and I found out that it would take more than a 2-hour information session to become a member. The class itself would take almost a year! Yes, there was an information card to fill out, but even that was two pages long and included dates and information that I didn't even know about myself. This was not going to be an easy process. If I truly thought that the Catholic Church was right for me, I had to be certain of it. I was not going to put this much time and energy into something that was just the latest whim in my life. Filling out that blue, double-sided information card felt like a momentous occasion in my life; I knew that it could possibly be the first step in a life-altering decision.

The Sacraments of Initiation

Confirmation is one of the seven sacraments in the Catholic Church, and each of the sacraments has a purpose. Cumulatively, the sacraments serve as a way for man to connect with God in a real, tangible way. We cannot see God, touch Him, feel Him, hear Him. This chasm between us and God makes it difficult for many to accept Him into their lives, so the sacraments, then, serve as a bridge to help us cross that chasm. He gives them to us as a gift that is administered by the Church, the guardian of our faith. Together, the sacraments help to mold and shape our lives within the Church, but to understand them fully, we need to understand the role that each one of them plays within God's plan for our salvation.

Looking at the seven sacraments individually, they can actually be broken down into three categories: the Sacraments of Healing, the Sacraments at the Service of Communion, and the Sacraments of Initiation. The Sacraments of Healing (Confession and Anointing of the Sick), as the names would suggest, focus on healing ourselves spiritually - even physically, at times. The Sacraments at the Service of Communion focus on passing the faith onto others: Holy Orders focuses on the world at large while Holy Matrimony, or Marriage, focuses on sharing the faith within the family. Meanwhile, the Sacraments of Initiation (Baptism, the Eucharist, and Confirmation) center on our personal faith - our relationship with Christ and His Church. The Sacrament of Confirmation, then, is an essential part of our Catholic journey. It completes the work begun in our Baptism and brings us into full communion to receive the Eucharist.

As I stated at the beginning of this chapter, the primary purpose of this book is to help bring people into the Church, and this happens through the RCIA process. The common denominator and end result is Confirmation and being fully accepted into the Church. For children who grew up within the Church, they will most likely complete this step as a teenager, but for those who did not grow up within the Catholic faith and decide to become Catholics later in life, like myself, Confirmation happens through the RCIA process. The requirements will differ from person to person depending on their background. Some will have to be baptized and others won't. For those who never did First Communion as a child, that will happen during the RCIA process, as well. If you are someone who is considering joining the Church, or currently going through RCIA, I hope that you will use this book as one of the primary roadmaps in your journey.

Laying of Hands

During the Rite of Confirmation, one of the key elements is the *laying of hands*. This is the act of the bishop, who is the minister of the rite, actually extending his hands over those being confirmed, a practice which dates back to the earliest days of the Church:

> *Now when the apostles in Jerusalem heard that Samaria had accepted the word of God, they sent them Peter and John, who went down and prayed for them, that they might receive the holy Spirit, for it had not yet fallen upon any of them; they had only been baptized in the name of the Lord Jesus. Then they laid hands on them and they received the holy Spirit. Acts 8:14-17, NAB*

Notice the importance placed on this sacrament by the apostles themselves. They saw the Sacrament of Baptism as the first step to becoming members of the Church, but they sent Sts. Peter and John to complete their initiation through the laying of hands. Also, remember that apostles were sent to do this task, and our bishops today are their successors. For that reason, bishops continue to be the ordinary ministers of the rite when possible.

The laying of hands is not exclusive to the Catholic Church. As a Protestant, I remember seeing pastors laying hands on those sent out to do missionary work and anyone who is officially being ordained as a pastor or minister. But this was not something practiced by the average Christian. Baptism, for many denominations, is the only ritual performed. Why do Catholics perform the laying of hands on all new members during Confirmation? If we look back to the passage from Acts 8, the Apostles were sent to Samaria to lay hands on the people there. Nowhere does it say that it was only for the priests and religious leaders. They went to perform the Rite of Confirmation on all those who had been baptized, both leaders and laity alike.

In the course of the Catholic Rite of Confirmation, the laying of hands is sealed with Chrism oil, which brings special blessings on us from the Holy Spirit. Finally, we see the true importance of this sacrament. As we look closer at the Sacraments of Initiation, we see that Baptism cleanses us of our sins, the Eucharist joins us with Christ, and Confirmation connects us with the Holy Spirit. By connecting with the Holy Spirit, we are allowing God to work in us and through us in ways that He never had before. Confirmation, then, is not just a rite of passage, or simply a requirement to become Catholic; it fulfills God's plan for our lives by completing what started at our Baptism. With the Holy Spirit within us, our whole world begins to change, and we can begin to see the world through the eyes of God.

Gifts of the Holy Spirit

When we receive the Holy Spirit during Confirmation, what happens exactly? Do we feel any different? Will we fall onto the floor and start having convulsions? Does the sky open up and light come pouring down? No, not usually. Emotionally, you may feel slightly different - it moved me to tears - but I didn't *physically* feel different. So if you don't feel any change, especially at first, do not feel bad. Often times the changes are subtle and happen over time. You may not even notice it happening until sometime later. The road in the rearview mirror sometimes looks clearer than the road directly ahead of us. The Holy Spirit has begun to work in us, even if we cannot see it on the outside.

The Holy Spirit does not come empty-handed; He comes bearing gifts. These gifts will aid us in our lives as Christians, helping us to live the life God wants from us. Following God's will can be difficult, and the seven gifts of the Holy Spirit can help:

> *These gifts are permanent dispositions that move us to respond to the guidance of the Spirit. The traditional list of the gifts is based on Isaiah 11:1-3: wisdom, understanding, knowledge, counsel, fortitude, piety (reverence), and fear of the Lord (wonder and awe in God's presence). -USCCA, page 205*

Quite the list. These are the tools we need to be an effective Christian, both inwardly and outwardly. On the inside we can use these tools to grow in our relationship with God by better knowing, understanding, and following His will. On the outside we will begin to reflect the qualities of Christ Himself, who was the full embodiment of each of these gifts. Through us the world will see the beauty of Christ.

Look at each one of the gifts. Notice anything? We are not promised material wealth, a healthy life, freedom from stress, or any other worldly gifts. Unfortunately, mainstream Christianity may sometimes offer these false hopes for our lives.

Faith in Christ is not a lottery ticket guaranteed to win. Accepting the Holy Spirit into our hearts does not guarantee us prosperity on a physical level but on a spiritual level. They are gifts meant to develop and strengthen our character, regardless of what situations life may bring. In good times and in bad, we will have the spiritual maturity to handle anything that comes, making these gifts far more valuable than our own weight in gold.

Not to be Taken Lightly

As I sat in my RCIA class, it was interesting to learn the various reasons why people were there. Many were getting married into the Church and wanted to be confirmed first. Others were already married and hoped to have their marriage blessed by the Church. Some had been attending Mass for years but had always put it off. I was one of the few in my class converting for the simple sake of converting. No motives, just converting. Whatever one's reason may be, God leads you into the Church for a reason. No one is there by accident. If God has willed you to be there, it should not be taken lightly.

Unfortunately, it does not take long to realize that some people are taking Confirmation too lightly. To them it is just fulfilling a requirement of the Church, nothing more. They fail to realize the true importance of what is happening in that classroom. They are on one of the most remarkable journeys we will ever experience, but they are blind to what is going on around them. Imagine flying on a plane for the first time and never looking out the window. One would completely miss the marvel that comes during take off and landing. During the RCIA process, life is finally taking off the ground; it would be a shame to miss it.

RCIA prepares you for the coming of the Holy Spirit. The Church is equipping you with the knowledge and resources that you need to be spiritually ready for one of the most pivotal events of your life. Moments like a wedding, birth of a child, or graduation can rank high on our list of fond memories. Our Confirmation should rank highly on that list, as well. What moment could be more important than the one in which you invite the Holy Spirit, wholly and completely, to come into your heart? The Sacrament of Confirmation is not to be taken lightly. It is one of life's most precious gifts.

A New Chapter

Before knowing much about it, I took Confirmation in the Catholic Church too lightly. I had already been through a similar process as a Lutheran, and as a long-time Christian, I felt that I had little to learn. Perception, however, is often vastly different from reality. I quickly learned how valuable the sacraments are to our lives, including the graces that come from Confirmation. Receiving the gifts of the Holy Spirit, whether I felt it at the time or not, has changed my life. Now I am better equipped to face life's challenges, and I can be certain that the Holy Spirit is always there to guide me.

Many see Confirmation as the completion of a journey, the purpose and goal of the entire RCIA process, but the truth about Confirmation is that it is only one step on a much larger journey. In fact, it is truly just the beginning of a new life with the Holy Spirit. When the RCIA chapter of our lives is complete, a new chapter awaits us. Becoming Catholic was a huge milestone in my life, but my adventures as a Catholic continue to deepen my faith even further. Through the guidance of the Holy Spirit, I pray that your voyage towards Catholicism brings as much meaning and purpose as mine did.

Chapter 10
Heavenly Conversations

Talking with God

One of the most difficult aspects of faith is building a relationship with an invisible God. We can read Scripture and other writings that point to His existence. We can see evidence of His work all around us, especially in the little miracles of life. We can come to believe that God exists, but having faith in the Lord requires a personal relationship with Him. You believe that I exist, but do you trust me? Do you have faith in me? Maybe, maybe not. But the people in my life that I know personally - my family, friends, coworkers - would, I hope, feel different. They trust me because they know who I am. They know who I am because of the things I do and the words I say, and it is the words I say, our communication with each other, that make the real difference. Our conversations help to build stronger relationships with each other. Why, then, do we skip this part of our relationship with our Creator? Talking with God through prayer is the key to a deeper, stronger faith, but in the course of our busy lives, it can often be overlooked. The Lord wants us to come to Him; He wants us to speak with Him. We have a God who is always willing to listen - we just need to make the time.

Praying in Darkness

I would love to say that prayer has always been a big part of my life, but that would simply not be true. Honestly, I continue to struggle with prayer to this day, and I think that it is something that I can always improve on. As a kid, I remember learning the "Now I lay me..." and eventually the Lord's prayer, but I don't recall how much or how little I actually said either one, which leads me to believe that it was not too often. Prayer was not common in our home, except at big feasts like Thanksgiving, Christmas, and Easter. Some people only attend church that often each year, and we barely prayed that often. Looking back, I struggled through most of my childhood to really know and understand God, and I believe that it was my lack of prayer that caused it. I was learning everything I needed to know about God in Sunday school, but because I was not actively talking with God, I failed to build a relationship with Him.

Even if we do not grow up prayerful, the idea and concept of prayer always stays with us - especially in the darkness. When life becomes difficult, and tragedies happen, we often turn to prayer. It's a shame, really. Instead of building a relationship with God on a daily basis, we only turn to Him when we are in need of a miracle. We use God as a crutch. If He doesn't deliver our miracle we use it as an excuse not to pray later. But how can we expect God to answer our prayers in times of need yet never offer Him prayers of joy? It's selfish. We are building a one-way, emergency-only relationship with God, and that is no relationship at all. Still, God loves each one of our prayers regardless of how infrequent they may be. He always listens to us no matter what. The Lord desires that one day, those prayers in the darkness will turn into so much more.

After years of denying God and not praying a single word, my life was in darkness. I was overcome by depression, and my life was spinning out of control. With my life literally on the line I turned to Him in despair. I wasn't sure if I believed in Him - I didn't even know if He existed - but I made a desperate plea for my life. Out of the darkness the Lord responded in a major way. Without Him, my life would have ceased to exist, but now I was given a second chance at life. After that my life began to change as I gave my life over to Christ. I learned that God will answer our prayers if we ask. While I am still not the greatest of prayer warriors, daily conversations with God have become a vital part of my spiritual life. Not only did prayer lead me to God, it has also helped me develop an intimate relationship with Him. Prayer literally saved my life.

Vain Repetition

Christ changed me from the inside out through our regular conversations. With the Holy Spirit's help I could talk to God whenever I wanted. My Christian faith began to develop, and my prayer life right along with it. The two went hand-in-hand. When my prayer life began to struggle, so did my faith. As one excelled the other did, as well. Personally communicating with Christ helped me to become the man that I am today. My prayers weren't full of *thee's* and *thou's*; they came straight from my innermost being. I talked to God in the same way that I would talk to anyone else. God knows what is in our hearts, and I didn't feel the need to use fancy words or repetitious language in my prayers. Each conversation was a unique conversation with my Lord and Savior.

Being formed in the nondenominational, evangelical tradition taught me that standardized prayers like the ones that

Catholics often pray are just vain repetitions. Prayers like these
were just overly robust language used to make the one praying
them feel more devout than they actually were. Yes, they were
Christ-centered, but they lacked emotion. How could people
say that they are having a conversation with God when they are
simply repeating a prayer they've said a thousand times before?
It made little sense to me. Real prayer was an outpouring of
emotions, not vain repetitions.

Of all prayers, the Rosary made the least sense to me.
Catholics did not just repeat a prayer once, they said the same
prayers multiple times. How could saying the Hail Mary fifty
times do any good? Praying to Mary was a challenge in itself.
Why don't Catholics just pray directly to God in the first place?
Mary - maybe, but the saints? Now I am supposed to pray to
other men and women? Not only was a Catholic Mass full of
repetition, week in, and week out, but also their daily prayers.
Was there anything about Catholicism that was not built on
repeating the same thing many times over? I saw little value in
it. If our faith is dependent on building a personal relationship
with God, standard Catholic prayers seemed to offer little help.

Skeptical Prayers to Saints

Years after becoming Christian, my life had spiraled out
of control again. A series of poor choices had led me to dark
times. During the years leading up to that point, my faith had
been put on the back burner, so I was lacking the peace and
comfort that normally came from God. Remembering my dark
times from years past, I realized that prayer was the answer. To
overcome the obstacles I was facing I could not do it alone. I
needed the help of the Holy Spirit. At the same time I turned
to others for help and emotional support, and my sister, a
devout Catholic, offered me a prayer card: a prayer to St. Jude,

Patron Saint of Lost Causes. I told a bit of this story in the chapter on saints, but it deserves some elaboration.

With nothing to lose I decided to say the small prayer on the back of the card. In truth, it went against everything that I believed: praying to saints, vain repetitions, and so on. But believing that my life may truly be a lost cause, I began to say the prayer every night before bed. In the chapter on saints I spoke about the benefit of having St. Jude praying on my behalf, but this little prayer offered a number of other benefits, as well. First and foremost, I was often at a loss for words. My life had spun so far out of control that I didn't know where to begin. My life was at rock bottom. My career was in shambles, I had very few friends, and I felt completely alone. When I struggled to simply find the words to say, when I couldn't even begin to express the pain in my heart, the words on the back of that card said everything I needed them to.

Another benefit that came from that card was that it became a regular part of my daily routine. After brushing my teeth and getting ready for bed that prayer was the last thing that I would do before going to sleep. I slept better each night with those thoughts running through my mind. I found peace in knowing that God was listening. For the first time in many years, prayer was becoming an integral part of my life. My faith was growing stronger because of a Catholic practice, a vain repetition, and I discovered that there was nothing vain about that repetition at all. My road to spiritual recovery began on the back of a prayer card years before I decided to become Catholic. I am now convinced that the prayers of St. Jude on my behalf, years before my conversion, were the beginning steps in my Catholic journey.

The Lord's Prayer

On the road to Catholicism, I had to overcome my own internal biases against many Catholic doctrines, including arguments against Catholic forms of prayer. One of the most common arguments against saying prayers repetitiously comes from Matthew 6:7, which states:

> *"In praying, do not babble like the pagans, who think that they will be heard because of their many words." - Matthew 6:7, NAB*

In other translations, these words are translated as "vain repetitions." This is directly where the term comes from. Jesus Himself made this statement. When looking at this singular verse on its own, one might begin to think that the argument seems pretty clear until you read what comes next. Two verses later, Jesus continues:

> *"This is how you are to pray:*
> *Our Father in heaven,*
> *hallowed be your name,*
> *your kingdom come,*
> *your will be done,*
> *on earth as in heaven.*
> *Give us today our daily bread;*
> *and forgive us our debts,*
> *as we forgive our debtors;*
> *and do not subject us to the final test,*
> *but deliver us from the evil one."*
> *-Matthew 6:9-13, NAB*

Of course, the translation may be slightly different, but any Christian can recognize that passage as the most famous prayer of all time: the Lord's Prayer, or as it is known by Catholics, the Our Father.

The most common objection to repetitious prayer comes just two verses, *two sentences*, before the Lord teaches us the Our Father. Why would the Lord contradict Himself in this way? Is that even possible? No, it is not. Opponents of Catholic prayer incorrectly use this verse and fail to look at the larger context of Christ's teaching. Some may incorrectly say that Christ simply gives us this as a model, but we should come up with our own words. If that is the case, why is there a similar example in Luke 11? Luke 11 is just a shorter version of the Our Father found in Matthew 6. It seems clear that Christ Himself had no issue with praying in this way. Contradicting the Church's model of prayer means contradicting the teachings of Christ. With that in mind, there seems to be no reason to doubt the use of traditional prayers.

Hail Mary

Looking back again to the chapter on saints, I discussed the role of the saints' intercessory prayers in our lives. Together, the communion of saints, both the saints in heaven and on earth, can have a powerful impact on our lives by offering up their prayers for us. The saints in heaven, especially, are closer to God than we are, so we would expect that their prayers have special favor with Him. And if their prayers hold a special place in God's heart, how much more does Jesus value the prayers of His mother, the Blessed Virgin Mary? The Hail Mary, then, is a cornerstone in the lives of many Catholics because it is the standard prayer asking for the Blessed Mother's intercession. And surprisingly, this prayer has more Biblical background than I had ever realized before. Let's begin by looking at the prayer as a whole:

Hail Mary, full of grace. The Lord is with thee.
Blessed art thou among women, and blessed is the fruit of
your womb, Jesus.
Holy Mary, Mother of God, pray for us sinners now, and
at the hour of death.
Amen.

Immediately, some will argue that we should not hail
Mary - that it's some act of worship - but the first line of this
prayer is actually a quote from Luke 1, when the Archangel
Gabriel speaks to Mary. In that verse, St. Gabriel greets her by
saying, "Hail, favored one! The Lord is with you" (Luke 1:28,
NAB). Other versions of the Bible translate this verse almost
exactly as we say the Hail Mary today. Already, we can see the
Biblical context for this prayer. It is a reflection of the
Scriptures, and if one of God's archangels hailed Mary when he
met her, I think that we can do the same.

The next line in the Hail Mary also comes from
Scripture. Later in Luke 1, St. John the Baptist was still in the
womb of his mother, Elizabeth, when Mary came to see them:

When Elizabeth heard Mary's greeting, the infant leaped
in her womb, and Elizabeth, filled with the holy Spirit,
cried out in a loud voice and said, "Most blessed are you
among women, and blessed is the fruit of your womb." -
Luke 1:41-42, NAB

Elizabeth was prompted by the Holy Spirit to say this! She did
not come up with it on her own. So far, the entire Hail Mary
comes directly from Scripture. Many will argue the use of the
Hail Mary prayer, but how can they argue the use of Scripture

in our prayers? Their argument is unbiblical, not the Hail Mary itself.

The last line, of course, is when we ask Mary to pray on our behalf. Like any other prayer to her or the saints, we are not worshipping her; we are asking her to pray to God for us. Her prayers have been known to lead to miracles. Why? Because of what we learn in Luke 1. Mary is full of grace, the one God chose to carry His Son. She holds a special place in His heart, and she should hold a special place in ours, also. The Biblical basis for the Hail Mary makes it a worthy prayer to say right along with the Our Father. Both prayers, rooted in Scripture, reflect the glory of God and serve as a guide to deeper, more meaningful prayer. I once questioned the validity of saying the Hail Mary; now I can't imagine my life without it.

Prayer Without Meaning

The danger with saying the same prayers repetitiously, whether it is the Our Father, Hail Mary, Glory Be, or any other traditional prayer, is that we may begin to forget their meaning. This is the argument of many Protestants, and to some degree, they have a point. If we begin to simply repeat these prayers without taking the time to reflect on their meaning, we will forget the significance of their words. The Church tells us in the Catechism:

> *The memorization of basic prayers offers an essential support to the life of prayer, but it is important to help learners savor their meaning.* -CCC, 2688

This passage references teaching children how to pray, but it can be applied to adults, as well.

As a convert to Catholicism, understanding the significance of various prayers was a valuable lesson for me to learn. Luckily, we've begun that process by already discussing the Biblical significance of the Our Father and Hail Mary. Other traditional prayers have their value, too. What prayer can praise God more than honoring the Trinity in the Glory Be? Or what better way can we say thanks to God than by beginning our meals by saying grace? Spoken without meaning, the words of these prayers mean very little, but by remembering to say them regularly and from the heart, they are a terrific way to incorporate our faith into our daily living. Communicating with God is an excellent habit to have, and many traditional Catholic prayers offer an easier way to make that happen.

Of course, we can expand on each of these prayers, adding deeper meaning to already wonderful words. Begin the day with the Our Father, and then, reflect on the day ahead. Finish saying Grace by adding the specific things you are thankful for. Ask for Mary's intercession through the Hail Mary; then name all of the specific intentions you have. Like any prayer, we can make it as meaningful or as dry as we choose. It is not these specific prayers that lack meaning; it is our intentions behind them. Say these prayers with all of your heart, and you will reap the rewards of God's blessings in your life. Say them carelessly, and you will gain very little. Your soul gives these prayers meaning, not the words themselves.

The Rosary

The Rosary has become a symbol for Catholicism itself. While other denominations may have prayers similar to it, Catholicism's Rosary, and the beads that go with it, are quickly recognized as a Catholic practice. There are images all over print and web media that show Catholics piously carrying and praying the Rosary, both in churches and public places. But what is so significant about the Rosary? Is it really beneficial to repeat the same prayers that many times? Yes. Actually, as we look at the Rosary, it sums up many of the topics that we have already discussed in one prayer, bringing together Biblical significance with heartfelt meaning. Without giving full instructions on how to say the Rosary, we can still learn some of the basics. It begins with the Apostle's Creed, a statement of our faith. It continues with a mix of the Our Father, Hail Mary, and Glory Be prayers. Combined, we are seeking God's help, asking for Mary's intercession, and offering glory to the Trinity. In between the sets of prayers, the decades, there are reflections on various aspects of Christ's life, or *mysteries*. While the Rosary is being said, we can add deeper meaning by reflecting on various special intentions from our lives. The sum of these parts brings together each of the most important aspects of prayer, which is why the Rosary has become a beloved tradition in the Catholic Church. Learning the Rosary may seem daunting at first, but it is a practice that will pay greater dividends than you could ever imagine.

Prayer Warrior

Still to this day my prayer life could use a lot of work, but I am a much greater prayer warrior than I have ever been before. With the use of traditional Catholic prayers, I have a quiver full of arrows at my disposal. I had once considered these prayers to be vain repetition. I once thought that they lacked any Biblical basis. But now I have learned to use these prayers as a strong foundation on which to build my relationship with God. Through constant prayer I have connected with God in whole new ways and brought deeper meaning to my faith. It all began with a simple prayer in the darkest of times, and I have learned to incorporate prayer into every aspect of my daily life, from the moment I wake up until the moment I go to bed.

Prayer is not simply something that we should do; it is something that we *must* do if we want to grow closer to our Lord, Jesus Christ. Take time to learn and memorize the traditional prayers of the Church. Spend extra time learning their meaning. Then, with a prayer arsenal of your own, you can begin training to be a formidable prayer warrior yourself - ready for any spiritual battle.

Chapter 11
Everyday Catholic

Going Beyond Sunday

When you first began reading this book, you may have been at a different point from where you are today, right now, in this very moment. You may have been a Protestant wanting to know more about the Catholic faith. You may have been a Catholic whose faith was nominal, at best. It is even possible that this book has been your first introduction to the Christian faith, and your life has drastically changed. Wherever you have come from, and wherever you may be, the next step in the journey is to take your faith beyond Sunday. While celebrating Mass on Sunday each week is an essential part of our faith, it is often what we do the rest of the week that speaks the greatest volumes about us. We cannot attend Mass on Sunday, walking around our parish with our heads held high, and then return to a very different life on Monday. Being Catholic goes beyond our Sunday obligation to attend Mass; it is a constant state of being. It is who we are. You've learned a lot about the faith in this book thus far. Are you ready to take it to the next level?

ChrEaster

Within the larger Christian church, spanning all denominations including Catholic, there is a large population or group of people whose religious practices distinctly identify them: *ChrEasters*. ChrEasters? Yes, ChrEasters - those Christians who only attend Mass or church services on Christmas and Easter. They are the precise reason that local parishes and churches have to add extra Mass times on those days. They are the reason that my normal spot is taken before I get there. But who am I to judge? During my childhood, showing up even on those days would have been a miracle. Regularly attending church was simply not a part of my weekly, or even monthly, routine, and as I grew older, nothing changed.

Why do ChrEasters choose these two days every year to go to church? Because deep down in their heart, whether they realize it or not, they know how important these days are in the history of the world. Christ's birth signifies God's unending love for us as He was willing to humble Himself and become man, and His death and resurrection shows us how deep that love truly goes. My faith as a child may have been weak at best, but I still understood that. The rest of society seems to understand it as well because these two holidays, especially Christmas, have forever shaped popular culture. We may not live in the most devout or pious times, but the life of Jesus continues to resonate throughout our civilization.

Each year, Christmas and Easter were the highlights of my year - not from a religious standpoint but a family one. I loved spending time with family on these days. The focus of the holidays has definitely shifted in modern culture. Over the past few years, I have even heard of various Protestant churches, primarily the more modern, non-denominational ones, that are no longer having services on these days. Instead of celebrating Christmas and Easter on that day, they are celebrating it the day or week before, so families can spend more time together - without church getting in the way. Sound absurd? I think it does. Instead of spending Christmas and Easter worshipping God, they are choosing to put the focus on the family instead. While I believe our families are important, our faith is far more important, and it is a shame that any Christian denomination would feel differently. Our world is already drifting farther and farther away from God. What will happen when ChrEasters no longer have a reason to attend?

Sundays Optional

After slowly fading from ChrEaster to completely rejecting Christianity, my faith was renewed, and I became *born again*. It took some time to find a church that fit, but I finally found one that was just my style: a modern, non-denominational church. Sunday services were more like a rock concert followed by an inspirational speech than a church service. It hardly resembled the old-fashioned services of my Lutheran childhood. It was exciting. It was fun. I *wanted* to attend. My attendance at Sunday services quickly became regular. I even attended the occasional midweek service. For the first time, I looked forward to going to church on Sunday. My life had drastically changed from former ChrEaster to Bible-thumping, church-attending, modern Christian.

Life, unfortunately, always finds a way to interrupt our best efforts. Other obligations would often mean skipping that week's service. My tendency to oversleep wasn't much help either. When I found a routine for attending church, things went pretty well, but as soon as that routine was interrupted, I quickly fell off track. My church attendance over the next ten years was full of peaks and valleys. I went from attending every week, no excuses, to not going for months, if not longer, at a time. There was nothing requiring me to attend, and my sloth and laziness often overcame the faith that beckoned me to go.

My faith in Christ remained strong, but my practice of that faith didn't.

I can look back over the years and see a direct correlation between my church attendance and my faith. When I attended church regularly, my life started to move forward. I prayed more, served more, studied more. However, during those times when my attendance began to slip, the rest of my life began to slip along with it. Prayer became almost nonexistent. Reading and studying the faith came to a halt. I switched my car radio back to the secular station instead of the usual Christian station set on my dial. Everything that normally defined my identity as a Christian began to fade into the background. No one was forcing me to go to church, but I should have forced myself. Would becoming Catholic give me the push I needed?

Precepts of the Church

Coming to the Catholic faith, I expected there to be more obligations and rules to follow. It was one of the aspects of the Catholic faith that had made me opposed to Catholicism for so long. Faith was about my personal relationship with Christ; it was about love, not rules. How could anyone's rules bring me closer to God? For years there was a large wall around my faith, protecting me from outside influences, but as I began to learn more about Catholicism, the wall began to crumble. I understood Sacred Tradition, the papacy, Catholics' love of Mary, and the beauty of the Eucharist. Maybe there was something to the rigid structure of Catholicism. Maybe the rules served a purpose. Being a ChrEaster didn't work, and neither did my weekly rock concerts. Could Catholicism change all of that? I decided to find out. Step one was learning what the rules are. Step two was deciding if I was willing to follow them.

There are many doctrines that help provide the structure and practice of the Catholic Church, and one of those doctrines, known as the *precepts of the Church*, gives five specific rules that Catholics *must* follow. These requirements are:

- Attending Mass on Sunday and Holy Days of Obligation
- Confessing sins at least once a year in the Sacrament of Reconciliation
- Receive the Eucharist at least during the Easter season
- Observe days of fasting and abstinence
- Help provide for the needs of the Church

If we look at the precepts, we have covered, or will cover, all of them. We read one chapter on the Eucharist, and one on Confession. This chapter will cover attending Mass and fasting, and the last chapter will cover assisting the Church. Everything you need to be a good Catholic, then, begins in these pages.

Are the precepts required? Yes. Along with the Ten Commandments and other doctrines, they help to define the very basics of how we should live as Catholics. Already, I know some may be running for the door. But are they actually that difficult? Confessing our sins once a year hardly seems to be a challenge. Giving God one hour per week doesn't either. We can make a lot of excuses as to why we cannot live up to these precepts, but it is only our laziness and unwillingness that keeps us from fulfilling these requirements.

Honestly, I was surprised at the detail of the precepts: the exactness of how often we should do this and do that. Why would the Church be so specific? In a way, I feel like a child with a list of chores to do before I can go play. Well, it's exactly that. The Church, like a parent, has laid the ground rules for our own benefit. They are not meant to punish us; they are meant to help us grow. Our parents required us to do homework. They warned us about touching a hot stove. They gave us rules to follow so that we could become a responsible adult. In the same way, Holy Mother Church gives us, her children, these precepts to allow our faith to mature. Look at the example of my life. When my church attendance slipped, so did my faith. My faith would have remained strong all of those years if I had simply attended church more. For that reason, the Church requires us to attend. Following the precepts may seem difficult, but the benefits will be worth our while.

Mass Requirement

"Mass is required?" That was my first reaction to learning the precepts, followed by, "Then, why do so many Catholics fail to go?" Good question. For the same reasons that I once had: other obligations that matter more to us than our faith. Soccer games, ballet recitals, family functions, job requirements, and a host of other excuses can quickly lead us away from our Sunday routines. Over time, our routine becomes *not* attending Mass. At that point it will take a radical shift in our life's priorities to get it back on track again. That is why the Church, through the precepts, requires us to go to Mass, and not just on Sundays, but on Holy Days of Obligation, as well:

> *You shall attend Mass on Sundays and Holy Days of Obligation. Sunday, the day of the Resurrection, should be treated differently from other days of the week. We do that*

in making the day holy by attending Mass and refraining from doing any unnecessary work. Holy Days of Obligation, when we celebrate special feasts of Jesus, the Blessed Mother, and the saints, should be marked in the same way. -USCCA, page 334

We'll spend more time discussing Holy Days of Obligation later, but for now, realize that the Church sees them as essential as attending Sunday Mass.

Looking at the Church's teaching, then, we see that the primary goal is to help us focus at least one day a week on our relationship with God. We are to treat these days just like holidays (notice the similarity between *holidays* and *Holy Days?*), so imagine celebrating one holiday per week. Sundays should be that significant. If we were to treat Sundays in this way, imagine what it would do for our faith. We could relax more. Spend more time with family. Focus more time on prayer and studying Scripture. Our faith would no longer be overshadowed by other commitments - but become a central part of who we are. Peace would be a reality. When you look at it in this way, the precept of attending Mass each week seems less like an obligation and more like the path to a happier existence.

Feast Days

Earlier, in Chapter 6 about saints, I briefly discussed the role of feast days within the Church. Basically, they are one way to bring our faith into our everyday lives - by taking the time to remember the stories and examples of history's most faithful Christians. The *United States Catholic Catechism for Adults* tells us:

The feasts and memorials of the martyrs and other saints

> *are occasions to praise God for their identification with Christ's Paschal Mystery. They are examples to us of love for God and others, of heroic courage in practicing faith, and of concern for the needs of others. -USCCA, page 173*

In other words, we can use their example of living out their faith daily to inspire us to do the same. Their heroic stories can motivate us to live closer to Christ each and every day.

On a daily basis, we celebrate the lives of various saints. They have feast days attached to some point of their lives, such as their birth or death. We do something similar in the United States when we recognize Christopher Columbus, Abraham Lincoln, and Martin Luther King, Jr. We take a moment to reflect on the impact they had on our culture and find ways to allow it to inspire us. Many saints are given to a particular patronage; in other words, they are a patron saint. For example, St. Paul is the patron of evangelists for his work spreading the Gospel, St. Francis de Sales is the patron of writers for his work with the written word, and St. Francis of Assisi is the patron of Assisi, Italy because, obviously, he was born there. Whatever may be close to your heart, a particular place or topic, there is likely to be a saint tied to it.

The focus, of course, remains on God, though. We are not worshipping the saints for the work they have done; we are recognizing their faith in the Lord - hoping to follow in their footsteps. Growing up in Chicago, every kid on the basketball court wanted to be Michael Jordan. They watched his every move on television and tried to model their own playing just like him. We can do the same with the saints. On feast days we are called to remember a particular aspect of their lives. We can focus our day on implementing that into our own lives. We can model our daily habits after the saints, which ultimately will draw us closer to God.

Holy Days of Obligation

Not all feast days are tied to saints. Some feast days are tied to the life of Christ - Christmas and Easter, for example. There are also multiple feast days that are given to the Blessed Virgin Mary whose life deserved honoring on more than just one day a year. Some of these feast days are so special that they have been made Holy Days of Obligation within the Church. On these days, we are required to go to Mass just like on Sundays. The purpose is to pause our daily routines to reflect on these important milestones within the Church. It is a reminder that some days hold a greater significance in our lives.

When I first learned about Holy Days of Obligation, my previous feelings about Catholic rules and requirements began to surface again. More obligations? We are already required to go every Sunday, and now I found out that there's more! You might be feeling the same way. Relax. It's actually only six days a year. One of them, you should already be celebrating. In the United States, they are:

- January 1: The Solemnity of Mary, Mother of God
- Thursday of the Sixth Week of Easter: The Solemnity of the Ascension
- August 15: The Solemnity of the Assumption of the Blessed Virgin Mary
- November 1: The Solemnity of All Saints
- December 8: The Solemnity of the Immaculate Conception
- December 25: The Solemnity of the Nativity of Our Lord Jesus Christ

Did you notice that Easter is not on the list? Well, it falls on Sunday already, so it is already an obligation. Other than

Christmas, which I assume you already celebrate by going to Mass, there are only five more days a year. And in many dioceses in the United States, the Solemnity of the Ascension is moved to Sunday - leaving only four extra days each year. I think you can handle that.

The Holy Days of Obligation help to shape our Liturgical Calendar. Certain days are already celebrated by mainstream Christianity, primarily Christmas and Easter, but there are plenty of other days to celebrate each year. Why should we limit the celebration of our faith, the most important part of our lives, to only two days per year? With a name like Holy Days of Obligation, the one word that stands out is *obligation*, but remember, the Church has made these rules for our benefit. Honoring the importance of Mary's life, the Ascension of Christ, and the lives of the saints are well worth our time. These people and events have shaped our Church and have played a pivotal role in where we are today. These days are more than just an obligation; they are a celebration!

The Liturgical Year

Beyond individual feast days, Holy Days of Obligation, and Sundays, the Church's calendar is divided into seasons. These seasons focus primarily on Easter and Christmas which is probably why our culture has held onto these two holidays most closely. We often see Easter and Christmas as single days on the calendar, but actually they are an entire season within the Liturgical year. Both Christmas and Easter have seasons of penance that lead up to them helping us to prepare our hearts for the celebration, known as Advent and Lent respectively. Basically, it is another way that the Church through the guidance of the Holy Spirit, helps us to bring our faith into our daily routines.

For most of the year, we are in Ordinary Time which, as it sounds, is ordinary. It is simply our regular practice of faith, with a mix of feast days in between. The year actually begins, though, with the season of Advent. Advent, believe it or not, is a season of fasting and penance much like Lent. Today few people actually prepare themselves this way. Instead, we spend more time in lines at malls, but I digress. Then we move onto the Christmas *Season* which happens after Christmas, not before. Next we go back to Ordinary Time for a bit before we enter Lent. Lent, of course, is the season of fasting and penance before Easter, a common practice among many Catholics. We finish Lent with the Triduum which is Holy Thursday, Good Friday, and Holy Saturday, and begin the Easter Season that Sunday. Finally, the year closes back in Ordinary Time again.

Looking at the calendar from a high level, we see a cycle of average, ordinary days until we near a significant holy day. As we approach the holy day we first spend time preparing ourselves through fasting and penance. With our hearts now in the right place we can actually begin our celebrations. These celebrations do not last for only a single day. These two days, Christmas and Easter, are so important to our Church that we actually devote ourselves to an entire season of celebration. The rest of the world may not structure their schedules like this anymore, but for us within the Church, our year focuses on these two central events in history. It's just another way that the Church helps to shape our everyday spirituality.

Everyday Catholic

Learning how to be a good Catholic every day of your life is easy: follow the precepts of the Church and the Church's calendar. We are given obligations and mandatory practices to follow, but they are meant to help guide us into a more devout life with Christ. From a distance it is a lot to take in. You will never remember every feast day, Holy Day of Obligation, and dates of the liturgical seasons. Don't worry, though. The Church, starting at your local parish, will serve as a guide throughout the year.

This chapter began by asking if you were ready to take it to the next level. We focused on how to practice our Catholic faith daily by following the precepts of the Church and the liturgical calendar. In the next chapter - the final chapter of this book - I am going to challenge you to take your daily walk with God outside of your personal conversations in prayer, outside of the four walls of the parish, and begin acting on your faith through service to the Church. You have learned the basics of the faith throughout this book and begun applying it to your own life. Now it is time to share that faith with others.

Chapter 12
The Next Step

The 80-20 Rule

There is an old thought in business that 80% of the results come from 20% of the people. Applied to a given church, parish, or local community, some will say that 80% of the work being done and 80% of the money being donated comes from 20% of the members. Truthfully, the numbers may be even worse than that. In a parish with literally thousands of members, why do we continually see the same few dozen people devoting their time, money, and talents to the Church? It's time to change all of that. If we want to continue to see the Church grow and thrive in our community, we need to get off our pews and into the streets. We must stop sitting back and letting others do the work - assuming there *are* others to even do the work. This book started out as a learning process, but now we've reached it's true goal: action. You learned why to trust and follow the teachings of the Church and its leaders. We cleared up some misconceptions about the Catholic faith. We spent time in prayer and re-devoted ourselves to weekly Mass. Now, in the final step, we must take action: living out our faith daily and spreading the Word. This small step for us, however, may be a giant leap for someone else.

Evangelical by Nature

Throughout most of this book, I have shared my background in the Protestant, Evangelical Christian world. For the most part this focused on the differences between my life as a non-denominational Christian and the truths I learned in the Catholic Church. I pointed out the errors in mainstream Christian theology and explained my reasoning for becoming Catholic. But for everything that I believe Protestants have wrong, there is one aspect of faith that they do exceptionally well: evangelize and teach their members how to use their God-given gifts for Christ. In many ways they do this much better than Catholics - in the Western world anyway. There, I said it. Fundamentally speaking, as Catholics, we can learn to more effectively evangelize by modeling the successful efforts of our Christian brothers and sisters. We may disagree with them on many subjects, but they do this very well.

What is the difference? What are our Evangelical brothers and sisters doing differently from us? It's simple. They share their faith. They are unafraid to share their love of Christ with the world around them. When the opportunity arises, they do not hesitate to tell someone about the difference Christ can have in their lives. As their name implies, they are evangelical by nature. Evangelizing and sharing the faith are a regular part of their Christian lives. Can Catholics claim to do the same thing? Do we share our faith as openly?

Of course, many Catholics are very open about their faith. Many of the people I have met and bonded with from my local parish are skilled at sharing their faith. In my work online as a writer and blogger, I have met many enthusiastic evangelists trying to share the Gospel with anyone who will listen. Unfortunately, Catholics like these seem to be the exception - not the rule. Throughout my life I can remember many Protestants telling me about the love and forgiveness of Christ, but unfortunately, I cannot say the same thing about many Catholics. If we want to rebuild the Catholic Church, this needs to change immediately. We need to do a better job of sharing the Gospel with a world in desperate need of Christ's love and forgiveness. We can be silent no longer.

Apologetics vs. Evangelization

Apologetics is a favorite topic among many Catholics. Some of the best-selling books in the Catholic marketplace are on apologetics, and many of today's Catholic theologians and speakers classify themselves as apologists. But what is *apologetics*? Many Catholics see it as the core concepts and teachings of the Catholic faith. This is true. In many ways, this book covers many of those same topics and can be considered apologetic in nature. However, apologetics, in the truest sense of the word, focuses on defending something. In this case, we are defending the truths of the Catholic faith. We are using rational, theological ideas to explain the various teachings of our Tradition. Obviously, apologetics is an important part of spreading Catholicism, but at the same time, we must not confuse apologetics with evangelization. There is a difference between defending the faith and lovingly sharing it with others.

When we use apologetics to share the faith, we are taking a defensive stance. Taking a defensive position only leads to one thing: an argument. Instead of openly sharing the beauty of our faith with someone, we often find ourselves in a debate over theological differences. This rarely works. For some, especially those who rely more on their mind than their heart, logical arguments defending the Catholic faith may be exactly what they need. Be that as it may, theological debates are much more likely to turn people away from Catholicism. Our goal is to bring them closer to the faith, yet all we have done is pushed them away. There is a time and place for apologetics, but when it comes time to evangelize, we can often leave our favorite apologetics book at the door.

A friend of mine, a fellow Catholic, shared with me his efforts to convert a young woman back to Catholicism. For years, she had been attending the same mega-church that I once attended. Over the period of a few months, he had many debates with her over their theological differences. He tried everything. He pulled out all of the apologetic heavy-hitters: John 6, Matthew 16, and a slew of other verses. Nothing seemed to work. Finally, she said, "Jesus loves me, and that is all that I need." That was his moment. She gave him the key to bringing her back home again. Instead of debating any longer, she just wanted to rest knowing that she had Christ's love, and that is exactly how we need to evangelize: with Christ's love. He needed to show her that she could find Christ's love in a much fuller way in the Catholic Church through the Eucharist and our wonderful sacraments. What happened to her? Did she convert? Regrettably, no. He had a difficult time seeing the difference between apologetics and evangelization, and until we, as Catholics, can do a better job of that, we are unlikely to achieve positive results.

Who, Why, and How?

As we begin to talk about evangelization, there are three main questions to answer:

- Who should evangelize?
- Why should we evangelize?
- How should we evangelize?

Most people's first question, naturally, is *why should I evangelize?* Is it my job? Aren't priests supposed to do that? We'll get to that later, but for now, while I still have your attention, let's focus on *who* should evangelize, and more importantly, why it includes *you*.

Regarding matters of the faith, we often leave the work for our bishops, priests, and deacons. We assume that they, as leaders of the Church, will handle everything - including evangelization. But that is not their role. Their role is to shepherd the flock. They may be in charge of growing and molding the faith of hundreds or thousands of people in their local community. That alone is a big enough task. If we assume that they are going to help grow the flock as well we are assuming too much. As I said before, it is their job to shepherd the flock; it is *our* job to grow it. Yes, you, me, and the family sitting next to you on Sunday are called to share our faith and grow the Church. In fact, we are in the perfect position to do it:

> *By Baptism, every member of the Church participates in Christ's role as priest, prophet, and king (which is understood in terms of being shepherd of his people). The laity do this in the context of their lives within families, parish communities, civic communities, and the workplace...*
>
> *The laity are in the unique position of being able directly to infuse culture and society with the Gospel.* - USCCA, page 134

Our bishops and priests spend their entire day shepherding a flock of faithful Catholics. They may not have much opportunity to interact with people outside of the faith.

We, on the other hand, spend a great deal of our time among non-believers. Through our personal and professional relationships, we have the opportunity to share the Gospel every day with the dying world. It is for this very reason that we, the laity, are called to share the beauty of the Catholic faith with the world. We cannot sit back and expect the leaders of the Church to fill the pews; it's our job! *We* are the evangelists of the Church. Any questions?

Empty Pews

So let's get back to the question that is on everyone's mind: *why should we evangelize?* In the Western world, we always need to know why. It begins at a young age - any parent of small children can attest to that. Sometimes, as parents, our answer simply needs to be, "Because I said so." In the case of evangelization, one reason to evangelize is that we are told to do so by Christ:

> *"Go, therefore, and make disciples of all nations, baptizing them in the name of the Father, and of the Son, and of the holy Spirit, teaching them to observe all that I have commanded you." -Matthew 28:19-20, NAB*

Jesus did not *ask* His disciples to share the faith with the world; He commanded them. It is an integral part of following God's will for our lives. As Christians, we do our best to avoid sin, follow Christ's teachings, and live up to God's commandments. The call to evangelize should not be any different. Christ tells us to "make disciples of all nations," and that is exactly what we must do.

As children grow, we move from simply saying, "Because I said so," to actually explaining the reasons why. As we grow and mature in faith, it helps for us to understand our reasons for evangelizing. The answer may not be that difficult to find. One look at the empty pews in many Catholic parishes will show us the reason. The Church around the world continues to grow, but in Western society, including the United States, attendance has dramatically slipped the past few decades. Modern evangelical churches are moving into stadiums while the Catholic Church in the United States is closing the doors on many parishes. Among other reasons, it is the result of a Catholic laity that has lost its zeal for evangelization. We have become spectators, instead of participants in our faith. We *watch* Mass on Sundays, instead of actively participating in the sacred liturgy. We are a large part of the problem, but with the right attitude, we can also be a big part of the solution.

This leads us to the real reason for evangelizing: to save lost souls. Evangelizing goes beyond filling pews and offering plates. We have been given this awesome gift of salvation through Christ, and we should not keep it a secret. It is meant to be shared. We came to the faith, at some point in our lives, because someone was daring enough to tell us about Christ. Whether it was our parents, a fellow student, a coworker, or a stranger off the street, we can only find faith if someone leads us to it. Now it is our job to do the same for someone else. You can make a difference in the lives of others through the seeds of faith planted through evangelization. Imagine your life without Christ. Do you want that fate for your friends, family, and coworkers? Of course not. So why do we even hesitate to share the Good News? When the next opportunity to share your faith comes along, do not let it pass you by. Let the Holy Spirit guide you and you might be amazed at what will happen next.

The New Evangelization

One of the popular buzz words in Catholic circles today is the *New Evangelization.* It answers our final question: *how should we evangelize?* But what exactly is the New Evangelization? Often times it is confused with using new media to evangelize, such as websites, blogs, social media, and other new technologies. They may be one of the tools that is used, yet the New Evangelization is something entirely different. Basically, the New Evangelization is an effort by the Church to re-focus itself on evangelization - beginning with you and me. The Church is challenging us as everyday Catholics to take our faith outside of the parish walls and into the world. For the Church to continue to grow it depends on the efforts of ordinary Catholics to do the work.

Before you run off to go grab your soapbox and begin preaching on the street corner, you must do something first: evangelize yourself. Yes, evangelize yourself. Our first step in the New Evangelization requires that we learn and grow in our own faith. Reading this book may have actually been step one. I hope after reading through these chapters you have a better grasp on what it means to be Catholic. We are not Catholic by birth or because our parents and family are Catholic. We are Catholic because we live out our beautiful faith in our everyday lives. We understand why we have a pope, venerate Mary, love the saints, and pray the Rosary. We do not simply follow rituals; we actively participate in the greatest religion in the world. So if you skipped ahead to this chapter, you must go back and read everything else now. If you did not understand something, re-read it again. Christ wants you to evangelize, but He wants you to gain the tools you need first.

The first step, once complete, makes the second step much easier. What is the second step? Go evangelize. Share the beauty of the Catholic faith with the world around you. The world around us is crumbling underneath the weight of selfish desires and sinful lifestyles. Now more than ever, society needs to re-embrace Christ as her Savior. We can help change all of that by simply exposing the world to the Truth. All we need to do is plant the seed and allow the Holy Spirit to do the rest. It's that simple. We need to allow the world to see Christ through our words and actions. Remember, someone once planted the seeds that led us here; now, we simply need to do the same for someone else. We may not bring thousands of souls to Christ, but if we can bring just one the effort would be worth it.

Different People, Different Gifts

Some of you may feel that the answer to *how we should evangelize* was not complete, and the New Evangelization does not apply to you. Some will say, "I cannot speak or write well, so I am not made to be an evangelist." I can understand that. Sometimes we falsely believe that the only way to evangelize is through the spoken or written word. We feel that we need to write a book, publish a blog, or stand on stage to share our faith, but most of the world's greatest evangelists never approach a stage. Instead, they bring a number of other gifts given to them by God to help share the message of Christ. Remember, although Christ's teachings and sermons drew large crowds, His actions first drew their attention.

How can we evangelize without a gift for speaking or writing then? By our actions. Look around the world at the work being done by the Church. A great deal of it is done by reaching out in other ways. The Church runs hospitals to care for the sick, molds our youth through universities and schools, and sends missionaries worldwide to care for the poor. On the local level we can do the same thing. We can volunteer at our local hospitals helping care for the patients. We can help mentor our youth as catechists or in youth ministry. We can care for the poor by spending time at the nearby homeless shelter or food bank. Believe it or not, caring for people in this way is one of the most effective means of evangelization. While speakers and writers may get the spotlight, the work done on the front lines of Catholicism is just as crucial to the mission of the Church.

There are other ways of supporting the Church without physically doing something. Prayer is one of the most valuable ways that we can help build up the Church. Our actions often focus on what we do for the Church. Prayer focuses on what God does. Like other ways of serving the Church, our prayers are magnified when more people lift up their voices to God. Regardless of any other methods that we may be called to serve the Church, every single one of us should be praying the Rosary, seeking the intercessions of the saints, and fervently asking God to give us the strength and wisdom we need to be good Catholics. Compared to other forms of participating, prayer does not require any special gifts, but there are different ways of praying. Some will devoutly say the Rosary daily. Others will spend hours each week in an adoration chapel. We can each find a unique way to support the Church as prayer warriors.

We have an infinite number of ways to participate based on our unique gifts. If you can bake, create some treats to raise money for your local parish. If you are good with tools, help with repairs at the local homeless shelter. If you are a good listener, spend time with those facing times of trial and depression. If you are a prayer warrior, say a Rosary or novena on the Church's behalf. Whoever you are, and whatever your gifts may be, the Church has a need for them. Don't believe me? Some think that it is easy for someone like me to say this. I feel comfortable behind a keyboard sharing my faith with the written word. I feel just as comfortable on stage letting the Spirit guide my voice, but these gifts are not everything. My wife, for instance, has an unbelievable gift of compassion. While I am great with words, she is great with people. She can use her gifts to reach people in ways that I never could. I can tell you about the love of Christ with big words and fancy prose, but she can show Christ's love in a very real, tangible way. Her actions speak much louder than words.

No gift is greater than any other. Actually, we do our best work as a Church when we learn to bring them all together. When we look at any well-run machine, there are many parts, each completing a different task. In a car, for instance, the engine is the source of power, the transmission converts the power into motion, and the wheels keep it planted to the ground. The same is true for the Church. Each one of us has a unique mission, and each mission is critical to the Church's success. With this in mind, take time to explore your gifts and find ways to use them in ministry. What can you do to help the mission of the Church? What can you do to evangelize the world?

Evangelical Catholic

We began this chapter with the 80-20 rule, saying that only 1 out of 5 Catholics is actively doing the work of the Church. The truth is that the number is probably far smaller. Imagine if we inspired more Catholics to share the Catholic faith with the world around them. We can learn a great deal from our Protestant and Evangelical brothers that empower 100% of their members to become ambassadors for Christ. It is time that we, the Catholic Church in the Western world, learn to become more vocal about our faith. We need to show the world the love of Christ through our words and actions. We need to remember the difference between apologetics and evangelization as well as recognize that we cannot win someone's heart through theological arguments. Finally, we need to get out of the pews and go evangelize.

For the past few decades, we, the Catholic laity, have lost our way. We have forgotten how or not been trained to evangelize, and some believe that it is not our responsibility. It's not too late to change all of that. Empty pews should motivate us to take a step in faith and share Christ's grace with our communities. By using our unique gifts and talents, we can be active members in the Church and help ensure that the Church continues to thrive for centuries to come. For 2,000 years, the Church has grown through the work of everyday Catholics like you and me. We can continue that tradition by being evangelical Catholics and answering the call of the New Evangelization. Are you ready to take the next step?

Conclusion

The End and the Beginning

Most nonfiction books start with the author's reason for writing the book, but as you can tell, this book is not like many others. Instead, I want to conclude where the beginning and end intersect.

For two years, I have worked on writing this book, and I am finally reaching the end. What I've truly learned, however, is that the end will just lead to another beginning. As I finish these last few paragraphs, I am reminded of where it all began. Slowly rewinding through my memories, I remember deciding to step out in faith and publish this book myself. I remember the sting of rejection letters. I remember two years of focusing my heart and soul on this book. I remember starting a small website to share my faith. I remember feeling the call to share my experiences with others through the written word. I remember the struggles I faced during my conversion to Catholicism. I remember where it all began, a college campus only a few hours away where I first understood the beauty of Catholicism. I remember the moment one man changed my life with a simple question, and I will never forget what he has done for me.

One Simple Act

A few years ago, my life was literally falling apart. I was

a single dad, freshly divorced, and my career was spiraling out of control. The military had sent my life on a rollercoaster, but my poor choices had only made it worse. My faith lacked roots and when troubles came my faith quickly dwindled. I was a grown man with little to show for himself. Just back from the military there were few that I could turn to - even fewer that I could trust. One man, my brother-in-law, Tom Nejmeh, stood out from the crowd as someone to turn to for help. Tom was successful in business, a devoted family man, and someone that you could always turn to in your time of need. It was one, simple act, though, that made the greatest difference.

Tom, had always looked out for me. As my mistakes began to pile up, he constantly offered advice and opportunities for growth. At the same time, he offered his time and energy, trying to cheer up a wayward little brother. One day, in an effort to lift my spirits, he asked me to join him at a Notre Dame football game. I wasn't a fan of Notre Dame at the time, but I couldn't pass up on the opportunity. Going to that game, though, had a larger impact than one would imagine. It was at that game that I first saw a strong, stable, devoted community of believers, and it was at that game that I decided to become Catholic. I was there for football, but God had so much more in store for me. My conversion story alone could take up many chapters, but my goal here is to share the impact of one man's decision to reach out in love and grace. Tom's simple invitation had changed my life.

Over the next few years, my life quickly began to turn around. My decision to become Catholic helped to solidify my faith in ways that I never expected. It was a continual growth process which led me to writing this book. I started dating the woman that would later become my wife, and I was close to finally finishing my college degree. For Tom, meanwhile, his life had a series of issues, primarily with his career. After years of success Tom's career began to struggle when the country fell on hard times. Eventually, he found himself unemployed with a wife and three kids at home. The pressure would be enough to break just about anybody. My life was picking up while his was headed in the wrong direction, or so I thought.

Just when Tom's career had hit rock bottom, he made an important choice: to use his talents in other ways. Tom began volunteering at various charities, spending his newfound free time to help others. He was busy handing out food at the food bank when he was unsure of where his own family's next meal would come from. Tom also found ways to get involved at his local parish, including the Knights of Columbus and other ministries, and faith began to take center stage in his life. Through this experience Tom had found a new direction. He recovered his career, but his faith continued to be his focus. Tom's struggles had led him to a greater purpose in life as it does for many of us.

A Greater Purpose

Just as I was finishing this final chapter, Tom was honored by receiving a *Family of the Year Award* from his local Knights council. About a week later we surprised him for his 40th birthday. After years of struggling with his career, Tom's life was coming together, and it had little to do with his finances. But in one of the most tragic moments I have experienced in this young life, we lost Tom suddenly - only one week after we celebrated his birthday. Tom had recurring heart problems that finally got the best of him. In a way, I like to think that his spiritual heart had more love than his physical heart could handle. His death stretched the limits of my faith as I lost the mentor who had led me to Catholicism in the first place. *How could I go on without the man that had done so much for me?* Unsure of what to do, I looked for a greater purpose to all of this.

Tom had always been a popular guy. His gift with the spoken word had led to his success in sales, but it also allowed him to connect with people. When it came time for his wake, people flocked to say their good-byes, and that line passing the casket continued for the next six and a half hours. I have never experienced anything like it. My sister, Heidi, Tom's wife, showed her strength as she greeted every person that came through that line. She stood by her husband's side to the very end bravely listening to each person. Getting a chance to listen to many of these stories myself, I was awestruck at the difference Tom had made during his short lifetime. My story was just one of many. Tom had made a profound impact on each of these people. His life had shown the greater purpose: each one of us can change the world through the smallest of actions - we only need to try.

Through Tom's life and death, I learned that everyone can make a difference. While he was never afraid to debate religion or politics, Tom did not preach. Instead, Tom showed the love of Christ through his actions. He lived his faith. He showed us that it is never too late to turn over a new leaf and turn your life over to Christ. Understanding why Tom died is almost impossible, but I can already see that God will use this tragic event for a greater purpose: to touch the lives of so many others through the stories of his life. My hope is that sharing his story with you will be just one small part of that.

The Journey Continues

My journey began the day that my brother-in-law invited me to a football game, and it continues today. He may be gone, but his impact will live on. Your journey may have begun with this book, but it will continue on, as well.

We began this journey by building a strong foundation on the Church, our Sacred Tradition, and by understanding the roles of the leaders within the Catholic Church. Next, we dove into the key characters in our faith, including God Himself, the Blessed Virgin Mary, and the saints - learning how each plays a role in our lives. We can't understand Catholicism without understanding the sacraments, so we tackled those next. Finally, we finished up by applying our faith to our daily lives through prayer, celebrations, and getting involved in ministries. With that, you have come to the end of this book, but not the end of the journey. This book should be just one step along your ultimate path towards Christ, and my hope is that you will share what you have learned with others. Our faith should not be kept secret; we should proudly wear it on our sleeves.

The focus of this book has been on learning more about the Catholic faith, yet I hope that it will lead you to something more. Knowing the Catholic faith and living it are two entirely different things. To be Catholic we have to understand the basic tenets of our faith so that we can go into the world and share the beauty of Catholicism with our communities. You now have the foundation needed to go beyond sitting in the pews on Sunday morning. You can use the knowledge you've gained to make an impact on the world like my brother-in-law, Tom, if even in the smallest ways. Faith should be more than a comfort in hard times; it should motivate us to action.

Waking Up Catholic

At the beginning of this book I told you about my childhood dreams - how I wanted to wake up one day as a policeman, soldier, or superhero. I did become a soldier. The policeman idea never worked out. My quest for becoming a superhero is far from over. When we grow older, our dreams change. As a self-avowed atheist in high school I never dreamt of waking up as a Christian. Life surprised me anyway. As a Christian I imagined many things, including the call to ministry, but I never dreamt of waking up Catholic. Now I do every day, and I'm proud to say so. Becoming Catholic has changed my life in ways that I never expected.

Waking up Catholic is a decision that we must make each and every morning. No one is born Catholic. We do not marry into the Catholic Church. We choose to be Catholic. Each one of us must accept Christ and His Church on our own. There is a lot to learn, and this book is just the beginning. There is a lot more to learn, a lot more to pray about, and a lot of trust in God to gain, but we have begun this journey together. May God bless you on the next phase of that journey. If you're not Catholic already, learn more about the RCIA program at your local parish. If you're already Catholic, look for ways to expand your faith. And for all of you, share the message of this book and, more importantly, the Bible with the world. Let the Good News of Jesus Christ flow from your lips and be shown in your actions. The world is primed and ready to experience the Catholic Church in completely new ways. What are you waiting for?

Made in the USA
Monee, IL
28 January 2021